THE
GREAT AMERICAN
CUSTOMER

☆

THE
GREAT AMERICAN
CUSTOMER

CARL CROW

ILLUSTRATED

HARPER & BROTHERS *Publishers*

NEW YORK *and* LONDON

THE GREAT AMERICAN CUSTOMER

Copyright, 1943, by Carl Crow
Printed in the United States of America

10 - 3

FIRST EDITION

I - S

This book is complete and unabridged
in contents, and is manufactured in strict
conformity with Government regulations
for saving paper.

To My Sisters

LORA *and* **ROMA**

☆

ACKNOWLEDGMENT

WHILE I am indebted to a number of people for assistance in the preparation of this book, my principal obligations are to my sisters, Mrs. Roy L. Beck and Mrs. Roma Crow Walters, both of whom have offered helpful advice and criticism and have done valuable research work. Others who have ungrudgingly aided me with their specialized knowledge are Paul F. Lienau of the Socony-Vacuum Company, Gilbert Loveland of Henry Holt and Company, R. E. O'Bulger and Miss Vera B. Wilson of the Eastman Kodak Company, Mr. Frederick T. Sisco of the Engineering Foundation, Mr. E. H. Thweites, Mr. E. H. Mapes, and Miss Jeanne McHugh of American Iron and Steel Institute, Mr. Herbert Hosking and Dr. Rosamund J. Webster of the National Association of Manufacturers, and Dr. F. M. Walters, Jr., principal metallurgist, Naval Research Laboratory, Washington, D. C.

C. C.

CONTENTS

✩

The illustrations will be found in groups
following pp. *18, 50, 114, 146, 210*

INTRODUCTION

AN AMERICAN CUSTOMER

THIS book represents an attempt to tell the story of the slow and often painful processes by which Americans, a nation of farmers and fishermen, have become the world's greatest masters of machinery. As the result of the work of generations of inventors, scientists, manufacturers and merchandising men, we have become the greatest manufacturing nation and enjoy comforts, luxuries and conveniences superior to anything the world has ever known. It is not the story of statesmen who wrote our statutes or of generals who fought our wars—nor of the gallant heroes whose names shine so brightly in the pages of our history. Theirs is a familiar story. It is in the main the story of the hard-working American whose principal concern in life was to make a fortune. It is, if you will have it so, the story of selfish men who thought only of their own interests in a competitive struggle for success. We have had more than our share of public spirited men—of those who preferred fame to fortune—of those who willingly sacrificed their own interests to the common good. Their influence has savored the life of every generation and of every community, but they were not the men who built the America in which we live.

The driving force has been found in the struggle of the individual for personal success. Unlike other countries where the scope of an individual's life was circumscribed by law and custom, the American never admitted any limitations to his

ambition. In the pursuit of these ambitions he learned ways
to make the soil more productive and made machines which
would multiply the strength and augment the skill of his
hands. The artisan was soon superseded by the manufacturer,
who made articles of utility more attractive in design because
they found a more ready sale. The merchants looked for
cheap production so that they could find a wider market for
their goods. Because we began our manufacturing when most
of our people were poor, success was achieved by making
articles which could be purchased by the poor and the moderately well-to-do. This made mass production inevitable and,
as will be seen, it started long before there was anything that
could be called mass consumption.

There was nothing necessarily altruistic about the motives
of these workmen, artisans, manufacturers and merchants.
Each of them was trying in his own way to better himself and
had no other purpose in mind. But the success of every invention, of every improvement in manufacturing or distribution
depended, in the end, on its appeal to the public, that is, to
the number of customers it would attract. No matter how
much time and work was lavished on its manufacture, no
matter how beautiful or useful it might appear in the eyes of
its maker, the merchandise, whether it was a thimble or a
motor car, was useless unless it filled some real or fancied need
—that is, found customers who would buy it.

In a sense everything that was sold for the profit of the
maker brought benefits to the purchaser as well. It would
be difficult to find anyone more penurious or self-seeking
than the Connecticut craftsmen whose generation was bisected
by the adoption of the Constitution. They made no pretense
of public-spiritedness but they elevated the living standards
of their neighbors and of many who lived in distant com-

munities. They invented and manufactured many little household appliances with the sole idea of finding enough customers to make the manufacture of the gadgets profitable. In
the proportions in which they made sales they lightened the
work of housewives, added to the comfort of homes and
created a desire for other conveniences. The humble potato
peeler, the improved rolling pin, the pants buttons punched
from thin brass sheets made their early contribution to our
high standard of living just as surely as the electric light and
the telephone which came later.

The progress has been constant, only retarded a little
here and accelerated a little there. Each invention and each
improvement in manufacturing or distribution has prepared
the way for the next. A chronological list of inventions and
machines which sprang from their immediate predecessors
would require a list of "begats" as long as those in the Book
of Chronicles. Our latest mechanical marvel is the great
cargo carrying plane. No matter who the individual designer
may be, this wonder of the air is the result of the work of
thousands of inventors, scientists, engineers and artists. If it
were possible to untangle the intricate web of history it
might be found that if John Fitch had not invented the
steamboat when he did, the giant airplane would not be a
reality of today but just a possibility of the future.

The American customer has been fortunate beyond all
others. His cost of living has been constantly lowered, his
standard of living improved. He has, from generation to
generation, been able to buy more with fewer hours of work.
New machines perhaps as yet undreamed of will be invented
and mastered to make living richer and less expensive.

For these benefits the manufacturer, the merchant, the
salesman, the advertising agent deserve to share the credit

with the scientist and the inventor. Scientists make discoveries which enable inventors to devise new machines. But it is the others who make and sell the merchandise to the benefit of the public. Without the incentive to make Franklin's electrical discovery the basis for the manufacture of some saleable merchandise, electricity might have remained for many generations little more than an amusing toy.

THE
GREAT AMERICAN
CUSTOMER

★

Chapter I

WE HAD NO CARRIAGE TRADE

THERE were only about three million of us—three million Americans who, after September 3, 1783, were free to earn money in any honest way that opportunity afforded and equally free to spend our money in any way we liked. It was on that historic but almost forgotten date that England signed a generous treaty with us formally and legally recognizing the independence of the thirteen rebellious colonies. The British army, which had remained in New York after the surrender of Cornwallis, sailed home before the end of the year. All the vexations of old restrictions on trade, manufacturing and navigation were ended. John Adams, who was one of the American negotiators, was not at all certain that freedom to do our own manufacturing would bring us any prosperity, and he managed to get the right to dry codfish on the Atlantic coast of what remained of British North America. While the treaty was under negotiation the codfish had been adopted as the symbol of the prosperity of Boston.

Here was a new market ready for us to develop—a market destined to become the greatest in the world—but at the time of our new freedom one of the poorest. Some Americans owned a great deal of land, but it was undeveloped and untenanted and brought in no revenue. There was no wealthy landlord class as in England and Europe. Naturally there were no important manufacturers, for manufacturing had been prohibited by British laws or severely restricted.

There were no royal or noble families—no carriage trade important enough to be taken into account in any market survey. A few wealthy shipowning families lived in great houses in New England seaports, but they continued to buy goods from England just as they had done in the past.

There was, in fact, only one large class of customers either for merchant or manufacturer—the farmers. More than ninety out of every hundred people lived on poorly cultivated farms, grew their own food, spun and wove the cloth from which they made their own clothing. It was by catering to the needs of this class of poor and unpromising customers that American manufacturing and merchandising has developed and prospered. The fact that the early manufacturers and merchants had to cultivate the trade of this one class of homespun customers gave them a point of view which has never been changed and which has made our industrial development different from that of any other country.

Let us try to picture this American customer of 1783 living on his small farm, usually surrounded by the forest. It was because of the richness of the virgin soil rather than his skill or industry that crops were successfully produced. His farming methods were little better than those of the Indians and, like the Indians, he found it easier and much more interesting to shoot game in the forest or to fish in the streams than to grow crops and breed livestock at home. The armed revolt against British authority would have been impossible but for the fact that every farmer owned a squirrel rifle and was expert in its use. He was, of course, without any of the modern tools and so could cultivate what appears today to be pitifully small farms. There are innumerable records in New England of farms of between twenty and thirty acres, half of which were pasture, one quarter woodland and the other quarter cultivated. No wonder corn and wheat and practically all farm produce were relatively much more expensive then than they are today. The farmer was lucky if he raised enough beans, peas, corn or other grain to last from one season to the other. He usually raised a few pigs, which meant nothing more than that he held the ownership in the pigs his sow had farrowed. The rangy beasts roamed the woods in search of fallen acorns and in the winter ate the bark off trees. All were scavengers of the vilest sort and pork produced under similar conditions today would not be passed by any health department. A hog weighing as much as two hundred pounds was remarkable.

The other livestock, cows and sheep, were better cared for, were allowed the hospitality of the barn and hay loft. If there were any children in the family there was a period of distress beginning with the time when the cow went dry and ending when she came fresh again. The sheep were of poor breed and the wool they produced would be used today only in carpet manufacture. This wool and equally coarse linen provided the clothing of the family, hand-carded, hand-spun, hand-woven and hand-tailored. Cotton cloth which was imported was too expensive to be worn by any but the very wealthy. Horses were not numerous. The heavy, slow-moving oxen were more useful in pulling the clumsy plow or in moving loads through areas that were practically roadless. There were no wagons—only a few carts with wooden wheels.

The standard-sized frame house appears to have consisted of a single room eighteen by twenty-four feet, a size mentioned frequently throughout colonial records and for several generations after independence. That size provided a large room by modern standards, but it was quite frequently the only room, with a low, windowless attic where some of the children slept. Here the whole family—often as many as nine or ten—lived throughout the year. Here was the place of giving birth and the place of death. It was also the place where all the household manufacturing was carried on—a crowded place, hot in summer and cold in winter and at almost all seasons permeated with odors ranging from unpleasant to foul. The puncheon floor consisted of roughly squared logs laid on the ground.

The most conspicuous as well as the most important object in the room was the great open fireplace on which all the food was cooked. (It was not until fifty years later that the first American pie was baked in that Yankee invention, a cook stove.) Some, but not all, of the huge fireplaces were equipped with Dutch ovens, a bricked-in aperture which could be closed by a door. A bright fire of well-seasoned pine would be built in the oven itself and fed until the proper heat had been obtained. The oven was then swept out and with the door closed retained enough heat for baking.

A fire once kindled in the fireplace was never allowed to go out but was kept burning from month to month and year to year like the flame over an altar in a Buddhist temple. But there was no religious significance to this procedure. If the fire was inadvertently allowed to go out, live coals had to be borrowed from a neighbor or a new spark kindled with flint and steel and tinder. Children soon became expert at banking fires with ashes.

The Dutch oven did not play as large a part in early American cookery as has been supposed. Its operation took quite a little time as well as skill. The housewife had too much to do to bother with elaborate meals, and she had nothing but the coarsest of ingredients. Much more commonly used were the pots of varying sizes which were suspended over the open fire. Corn meal mush was a staple. Beans, peas, fresh vegetables, game and salt pork all went into the pot. Potatoes were sometimes roasted in the hot ashes, but potatoes were not common and were looked on as something of a delicacy. A kind of corn bread was produced by tilting the filled baking pan toward the open fire. The housewife, who had many duties to attend, did not cook three meals a day nor did she necessarily cook a fresh meal every day. The cooking pots were large enough to hold provisions for several days, or a week, and in most cases the contents of one pot were devoured before the next was put on the fire. In many households the whole culinary process was based on the theory that any foodstuff boiled in a pot was edible. The food on which the average American farmer lived would cause a riot in any modern penitentiary. Throughout colonial biographies one occasionally finds some prominent citizen characterized by his fellows as "amiable." This characteristic was notably uncommon and, it would be reasonable to suppose, was applied only to those with stomachs so valiant as to withstand the indigestible Colonial food. It was not until a generation after the invention of the cook stove (1830) that amiability as a characteristic of men in public life was taken as for granted and the adjective was dropped from biographical sketches.

There was always a spinning wheel in the room and sometimes a loom. Clothing of the poorest and coarsest sort was much more expensive than it is today. The development of machine-made textiles had just begun, and cloth of all kinds cost three to five times the present prices. No farmer could hope to earn enough money to buy clothing for his family and they were all dressed in homespun or skins or not at all. If there were any candles in the house, they were homemade. Tallow dips took hours to make, sperm candles were too expensive for any but the rich or for use in the meeting house. Therefore the only artificial illuminant in many homes was provided by the flame of the open fire. This could always be augmented by splinters of pitch pine stuck in cracks in the hearth where they burned brighter than any candle.

The housewife freed the wool of its grease by soaking it in urine. She carded, spun and wove the cloth, dyed it and fashioned it into clothing. In the summertime she did the gardening. She also made soap, but there is no evidence that the institution of Monday wash day had been established. Life was not simple but extremely complex, for the farmer and his wife had to be masters of a dozen trades.

It was a rare house that possessed chairs enough for everyone. It was taken for granted that children should sit on stools or benches, just as it was taken for granted that they should eat off their parents' plates. A communal drinking cup was the rule rather than the exception. Few families possessed any chinaware or glass. Wooden trenchers were commonly used. These were blocks of wood about a foot square, hollowed out in the middle. There was such a dearth of ordinary humble articles that it was not uncommon for a man to mention a pewter bowl, a pair or scissors or linen sheets in his will. The wool curing process, like all other home manufacturing, was carried on in the communal room and the covered vat provided a seat for one of the children. Another odorous receptacle in the room was the salt pork barrel. Hams and bacon hanging beside the mantel piece added their contribution to the odors.

As soon as children began to grow up and become curious about the facts of life, the married couple had to add a bedroom to this communal chamber or install a four-poster bed. Since the latter cost less, a great many of them were made. It was only when concealed behind the curtains of this bed that the fathers and mothers enjoyed any degree of privacy. An heirloom four-poster does not, as many believe, always indicate the opulence of some revered ancestor, but often the reverse. Many of these beds were not four-posters at all but just cubicles built inside the room, the sides covered with rough boards.

It is fortunate for the marriageable young ladies of the period that no such soul-scorching phrases as *halitosis, body odor*, and *tattletale gray* had been introduced into the sedate English language. With dentrifices and bathtubs completely absent, there can be no doubt that the daintiest New England maiden was, by present standards, always decidedly spicy in odor.

It was many years after the end of the Revolution before that English symbol of aristocracy, the bathtub, was accepted as something that could be fitted into the democratic way of life. During this period the greatest contribution to personal cleanliness was the "wash room," a cubicle between the main building and the out buildings. Here there was, in well appointed houses, a pail of water with a gourd dipper, a wash basin, a bowl of homemade soft soap and a towel. Those who were finicky enough to want to wash their hands before they ate were provided with the opportunity to do so. That was the early predecessor of the powder room and the guest towels of today. It was not until 1850 that a bathroom was installed in the White House.

From checking over the possessions and the needs of this typical family of consumers of 1783, it is obvious that a merchant or manufacturer would require the trade of a great many of them if he expected to make a fortune, for individually they bought very little. Still less cash changed hands, for there was very little money of any kind in circulation and its place was taken by an intricate system of exchange and barter. Grain was taken to the mill where the farmer helped grind it and paid the miller a toll of one-fourth to one-third of the meal or flour. Salt, about the only foodstuff that was not produced on the farm, had to be bought for use in curing pork and for the cattle; it was very expensive, costing from ten to twenty times the prices which have prevailed during the past half century. Children liked molasses on their corn bread but that didn't necessarily mean that they had to be humored. Coffee was as scarce as champagne is today, nor was tea as common as it generally was supposed. No available statistics of the importations of tea indicate any large per capita consumption.

The articles of furniture were usually homemade and, like the pots and pans on the hearthstone, were supposed to last a lifetime. As a matter of fact, they usually lasted through several generations. Although every housewife could spin, some could not weave or did not own a loom. In such cases the yarn was woven on terms similar to those of the miller. The wearer kept part of the yarn. Buttons had to be bought but they were used over and over again, and no one but the comparatively well-to-do town people bothered about buttons matching. Needles and sewing thread had to be bought, also the pots and kettles. The farmer made most of his tools for his farm work but in his capacity as carpenter and Jack-of-all-trades he had to buy hammers, saws, chisels and other hardware.

Shoes were a problem—a seasonal problem, for they were not essential in warm weather. The farmer often met this problem halfway by tanning his own hides, and the odor of tanning vat in the living quarters competed with great success over those of the dye pot, the salt pork barrel, the manure pile and the privy, if there was one. An itinerant shoemaker would cut and peg and sew this rough leather into shoes. Each pair of shoes was made to order, but that does not mean that they were fitted after the manner of expensive custom-made shoes of today. The shoes had to be large enough to get your feet into but not so large that you would step out of them when walking. It was not until the turn of the century that anyone thought of shaping shoes differently for the left and the right foot and another twenty years passed before any but the most fastidious dressers insisted on this distinction. The word *cordwainer* is now listed in the dictionaries as archaic. It was in common use in 1783, and everyone knew that a cordwainer was a kind of shoemaker who made moccasins. A great many people wore moccasins, which were easier to make.

Not only did the typical American customer need very little, but he did not make enough money on his farm to pay for what he needed. Cash revenue from farming operations could not be depended on. There were not many city dwellers, but even these usually kept a cow, raised chickens and pigs and maintained a kitchen garden and a few fruit trees. The sale of such farm products as eggs, fruit and fresh vegetables to city dwellers did not become a source of revenue until the towns grew much larger and more congested.

In order to get money to pay the taxes and buy the few necessities, the farmer usually had one or more additional occupations. He was not a good farmer but his abilities could not be judged on that accomplishment alone. His wife was a poor cook but she was in addition a worker in wool and flax, a dyer, soapmaker, candlemaker, etc. The husband was something of a carpenter, blacksmith, tanner, trapper and curer of furs—something of a Jack-of-all-trades, one or more of which could be depended on to bring in some ready cash. One of the common occupations was making nails.

Pelts of wild animals provided some revenue as they still do in many parts of the country. The trapping of beaver was so profitable that it was soon played out in many parts of the country. A more dependable source of forest revenue came from what was known as "pot ashes," later simplified to the one word potash. The method of manufacture was very simple. The manufacturers went into the forest, cut down the timber and, after it was seasoned for a few months, burned the logs and collected the ashes. These were leached into lye by the filtering of water, the lye boiled in a pot until it became a solid or semi-solid mass. This was a product of considerable value which could be profitably shipped long distances. That was not true of tan bark and charcoal, two other forest commodities so bulky that they could only be sold in the neighborhood of production. Many young men with plans to set up homes for themselves spent one or two winters in the forests making potash in order to earn enough cash to build a home for their brides. Many others about the turn of the century employed the same method to earn enough money to start some small factory or business enterprise.

It was on the scant trade of these early customers that the industries of the country were founded, and on the constantly increasing trade of their descendants that these industries have grown and prospered. The sons and grandsons of the few wealthy men in the new United States were not, with few exceptions, pioneers in manufacturing or merchandising. Perhaps some of the snobbish English contempt for the "tradesmen" deterred them, or perhaps their imaginations were not stirred by the prospect of great fortunes to be made from petty transactions. They invested their inherited money in real estate, banks, shipping and insurance, followed occupations that bore the insignia of wealth.

Leadership in the industries which were later to become so great was assumed by the sons and grandsons of the poor farmers who raised big families in crowded and foul-smelling houses. When they started to manufacture goods for sale to their new and rapidly growing country they did not think of John Hancock, George Washington, Robert Morris and the few other wealthy men of the country. There were few of them and they lived in remotely scattered areas. The customers they had in mind were of the same class and generation as themselves, descendants of men who worked their farms inefficiently and made nails and potash in order to earn a little cash.

Because the carriage trade was not important enough to cater to, because the only large group of customers consisted of men and women who were poor or only moderately prosperous, American manufacturing and merchandising started at the bottom. Success was only to be found by catering to the needs of the common man. This meant the mass production of goods to be sold in quantity at the cheapest possible price. The best artisans in England or Europe had their attention fixed on the wealthy trade—the prince or rich landlord whose patronage alone would keep them in business and possibly make them wealthy. The American artisans who later became manufacturers had to think of securing the trade of a hundred or a thousand customers in order to enjoy the same sense of security. As the years passed and their undertakings grew, the number of steady customers they required grew to hundreds of thousands, millions and finally, or presently, to tens of millions.

It wasn't until we had a head start in manufacturing that other nations woke up to the fact that the carriage trade was one of vanishing importance.

Chapter II

THE BIRTH OF INDUSTRY

OF THE thousands of colonial patriots who wrote pamphlets and made speeches about the English prohibition of manufactures there were very few who had an inkling of how to manufacture anything in the way of saleable merchandise. About the only things made in the colonies were such crude items as hand-woven cloth, handmade candles, handmade tinware and hand-forged nails. The English prohibition against colonial manufacture had been a constant irritant and eventually became one of the causes of war. But if all prohibitions had been removed colonial manufacturing would probably not have given the English manufacturers any embarrassing competition. While we had tailors, blacksmiths, clockmakers and cabinetmakers who executed orders placed by customers, they were, in most cases, men of much less skill than their fellow craftsmen in England.

There were also fewer of them. William Penn, Oglethorpe and other promoters of immigration to the colonies had been unceasing in their efforts to induce artisans to come to the new world. They do not appear to have been very successful, however, for the appeals never ceased and we began our national existence with very few skilled workmen and no ambitious plans for the development of industries. There were a few—a very few people who were enthusiastic about the prospect of manufacturing, but a great many more looked toward fortunes to be made in shipping. We had plenty of able seamen and many ships which had been made idle by the end of the war.

Although the subject was not mentioned in the text, the treaty of peace brought to an end what had for eight years been our most profitable industry, that of legalized piracy, known as privateering. Every master of an American ship was legally authorized to prey on British shipping and seize British cargoes which became his property. Thus piracy became a patriotic duty as well as a highly profitable enterprise. In fact, this phase of the war effort had a much stronger appeal than fighting in the field. During most, if not all, of the years of war there were more men engaged in privateering than there were carrying rifles in General George Washington's armies.

Salem, Massachusetts, was the principal headquarters of the privateers who with their small swift sailing ships ranged far afield, bringing in captured cargoes which found a ready sale in New England. Sometimes mistakes were made, for not all the ships that were scuttled and their cargoes pilfered were British. The business was so profitable that ships were specially built for the trade and the profits laid the foundation for many an aristocratic fortune. It was cold comfort to those respectable buccaneers to know that if they wanted to devote their time to codfishing they could dry their fish on British shores. Many of them drifted into the slave trade.

While a few laid plans to supply our needs by setting up local manufactures, many more made venturesome voyages to bring from distant ports articles to replace those we had formerly bought from the English. The *Empress of China* went to Canton in 1785 and brought back a cargo of Oriental merchandise. A year later the *Grand Turk* sailed into Boston with bolts of jeans, finely woven cotton, silks, porcelain, coconuts, monkeys, malacca canes, and cages full of Java sparrows. It was from such imported cargo as this that the shops of Boston, New York and Philadelphia, but especially Boston, were stocked. This Chinese merchandise was better than any the Bostonians had ever seen before and provided patterns and standards of workmanship and design which were to be followed by American manufacturers for many years to come. The cloth from China was hand-spun and hand-woven as in America. But the cotton threads were finer, the weaving more uniform. Paul Revere was struck by the beauty and simplicity of the pieces of porcelain and promptly copied them in silver. They were later copied by our early porcelain-makers and so have been handed down to us to this day. No one in America could produce articles like these, which sold at lower prices than our coarser products. Thus the daring and enterprise of our skippers served to discourage the development of manufacturing. Profits from sailing ventures were always brought back in the form of goods rather than cash. A great many people were ready to believe that we might better continue to be farmers and fishermen and buy our manufactured articles wherever the best market could be found.

The English manufacturers were determined that this should be the role we should continue to play. That was the age of monopolies and special privileges and trade restrictions which killed or stifled competition. The prohibition of colonial manufacture was only one of many forming an intricate network of British economy. Certain parts of England had a monopoly on certain trade and some manufactures and importations. When British merchantmen brought back from the Indian port of Calicut a beautiful cotton cloth which later became known as calico, the British woolen merchants were thrown into a panic. This cloth was so beautiful and so cheap that they foresaw the ruin of their own industry if faced by this competition. Parliament readily complied with their demand that the importation of this textile be banned and the manufacture of cotton be prohibited. The only use that could be made of cotton in England for many years was in the manufacture of candle-wicks. English traders, however, were allowed to bring cargoes of calico to the colonies.

As soon as the British manufacturers saw that their old monopoly on trade with the colonies was nearing an end, they devised new regulations which Parliament promptly legalized. At this time they led the world in almost all lines of manufacturing and especially the important one of textiles. The invention of the spinning jenny and an improved loom and the application of power to many of the mill operations had in less than a generation replaced the old hand methods and enabled the millowners to produce cloth at a fraction of the old cost. This industrial revolution brought the millowners of Manchester, England, a prosperity which made them rather dizzy, a prosperity they were prepared to defend against all competition. They felt sure of their ground. No one outside of themselves and their own workmen knew the design of their machines nor had the skill to operate them. Parliament enacted new laws designed to protect this monopoly. Heavy fines were provided for the exportation of any of this precious machinery or for the emigration of any skilled factory workers. As an added precaution, the factory owners placed their workers under bond not to tell any prying Yankees anything about factory operations or show them any of the machinery. Every factory was guarded as closely as a Masonic lodge. We continued to buy cloth from England just as in colonial days.

It irked the citizens of the new republic to be dependent on the old country for cloth, and various states offered rewards for the invention of textile machinery. For example, as early as 1789 the legislature of Pennsylvania offered £100 to anyone who would invent a power carding machine. These were actually offers of bribes to Englishmen to bring in designs of the machines which were operating so successfully in Birmingham.

Attempts to encourage the manufacture of textiles went farther than the mere offer of rewards for the invention of machinery. The sheep were of a poor breed, the wool coarse. One of our early diplomats is remembered principally because he succeeded in smuggling a few pure-bred sheep out of the country to which he was accredited. In some communities the butchers cooperated with their fellow citizens in a sustained campaign to increase the available supply of wool. The butcher agreed to slaughter no lambs and the people agreed to eat no mutton less than two years old. In many cities companies were organized to purchase spinning wheels and looms to be operated by "indigent females" of whom there always appeared to have been an abundant supply. Prizes were offered for the best made home-spuns, as well as bounties in cloth produced. Little children were taught to help in both spinning and weaving. The process of making clothing by hand was so tedious that the use of child labor was well nigh unavoidable. A great many attempts were made to build machines which would work like those of Lancashire, England, but none succeeded, and various states offered even larger cash prizes and bounties to anyone who would invent and build textile machinery.

These offers came to the attention of Samuel Slater, who was just then completing his apprenticeship in one of the English mills which was making cloth for the American market. The technical knowledge he was mastering was what was needed in America, and he felt that if he could cross the ocean and establish a mill he would soon be as wealthy as his employers. He did not attempt the rather dangerous venture of smuggling the plans for textile machines out of England, but in his years of work he carefully memorized them. Posing as a farm hand, he emigrated to New York, where he landed the latter part of 1789. The following year he interested William Almy of Pawtucket, Rhode Island, in his plans and actually constructed a successful machine from memory. In 1801 he built a factory at Rehemoth, Massachusetts. With his brother John he established in 1806 the industrial town of Slaterville, Rhode Island. He also started the first Sunday School in America. He is generally referred to as "the father of American manufacturing."

The first factory wheels in the country were turning and in every state, but especially in New England, men with a little capital were dreaming of the fortunes to be made by building spinning mills and carding mills which would replace the expensive old hand methods. England was the repository of all these skills, the only place where these wonder working machines were made. All of the inventive genius of England seemed to be devoted to textile machinery, which was constantly being improved. Slater's mills, by Manchester standards, were out of date before they began operation.

He had shown how textile mills could be established here, and other pillars of the church began purloining English trade secrets. Those who were interested in manufacturing

William Scott,

At his Store, North-Side of Faneuil-Hall, next Door to the Sign of General Wolfe, has just opened a large Assortment of the following Goods, which will be sold by Wholesale and Retail (for Cash only) on the most reasonable Terms ;

YARD wide, 7-8 & 3-4 Irish Linnens, from 10s. to 50s. O. T. per yard, 9-8 wide Sheeting from 12s. to 16s. per yard, 7-8 Dowlas, Diaper Table Cloths, Clouting Diaper and Huckabuck, Manchester Cotton Checks and Handkerchiefs, Jeans and Pillow Fustians, Jersey knit Stockings, Forest Cloths, Plains and Kerseys, Manchester uncut Velvets, 7-Thread Lastings, &c. &c.

TO BE LETT, BY
Thomas Wood, *of Salisbury,*

A Large and commodious House, situate at the Ferry in said Town, with a good Shop or Out-House, with two Barns, and Forty Acres of Land, the most Part adjoining said House ; the Remainder within half a Mile. Said House has been improv'd as a Tavern for many Years.   Salisbury, October 22, 1768.

A THEFT.

WHEREAS on the night of the 16th of this instant, the shop of the subscriber was broke open, and many articles as mentioned in a late paper, was stolen. The person who committed the fact, is discovered to be one William Lindsey, formerly belonging to Dudley, and has been discharged from one of his Majesty's goals in the county of Essex, where for theft and forgery, he has had his ears crop'd ; for which reason he wears his hair hanging down on both sides to his cheeks, is about 22 years of age, of a good stature, light hair, a little upon the sandy, fair complexion, and a little freckled, he past thro' Lunenburg the 18th, without any of the goods he stole, except a glass quart bottle ; it is probable he has secreted the goods ; he oftentimes calls himself Keyes, sometimes Samuel Homes ; he says he came from Pomfret, where he had his shop broke open, and that he is in quest of the thief. He had on a light-coloured cloth coat, striped shirt, leather breeches, and a pair of new shoes. Whoever will apprehend the said William, so that he may be bro't to justice, shall receive TEN DOLLARS Reward.

Leominster, Sept. 28, 1768.   THO. LEGGATT.

SIX DOLLARS REWARD.

RAN away October 1, 1768, *from the Rev. Mr. Paul Coffin, of Narraganset No.* 1, *in York County, James Fitz Gerald, an Irish Apprentice, of about* 18 *or* 19 *Years. He is a flocky thick Fellow, has a broad Face, and is not very Tall. He wears his own good black Hair, has had the Small-Pox, and speaks broken English. He had on and with him at his Departure, a Wool Hat, an old whitish Fustian Coat, dark blue. or greyish Cloth Jacket, Horn Button; and white Lining, two Pair Breeches black Cloth and light Purple Plush, two Pair Stockings blue and grey. two Pair Shoes; large Brass Buckles, a Brass Comb, and Watt's Spiritual Songs for Children, and a Book intitled, An Introduction for the Indians, in the Form of a Dialogue between a Missionary and an Indian. Six Dollars are offered to any Person who may take up and convey said James to* Nathaniel Gorham, *Merchant, of Charles-town, or to Major* Joshua Coffin, *of Newbury, or Doctor* Abiather Alden, *of Saco-Falls.   Attest.*

Narragansett, No. 1, *Nov* 1, 1768.   PAUL COFFIN.

Boston. Printed by EDES & GILL, in Queen-Street. 1768.

TO BE SOLD,
BY PUBLICK VENDUE,
On THURSDAY the 29th Inst.

At 3 o'Clock, P. M. if not sold by private Sale before. A Commodious Brick House, having four Rooms on a Floor, with a roomly Yard and Garden, and a Store adjoining, very agreeably situated on the Corner of two pleasant Streets, a little to the Southward of Dr. Cutler's Church, (being Part of the Estate of the late Capt. *John Aves,* deceas'd). Likewise a House Lot situate in Lynn Street, opposite Capt. *Hart's* Shipyard : For further Particulars, enquire of,   JOS: TURELL, Executor, &c. Who has to sell, Choice TABLE FISH, the best of SWEET OIL, WINES, &c. &c. &c.

LOST from a Lady's Side on Saturday Morning last, an outside Case of a GOLD WATCH, the upper Part peirced, the Bottom wrought : Whoever has found the same, and will bring it to Mr. *Benjamin Hallowell's,* shall receive half a Guinea Reward ; if offer'd to be pawn'd or sold, it is desired it may be stop'd, and Information given as above.

For GLASGOW, The Ship GLASGOW, *JOHN DUNN,* Master, Will sail with all convenient Speed. For Freight or Passage, apply to the Master on board said Ship, lying at *John Hancock,* Esqrs; Wharf, or to *Robert Gould's* Store, near the Mill-Bridge.   December 3, 1768. *N. B.* A Quantity of Choice Scotch COALS to be Sold on board said Ship, if apply'd for immediately.

ANCHORS and Blacksmith's Tools, Cooper's and Carpenter's ditto, Oyl Searchers, Smoke Jacks, Spades, Iron Shovels, and Bath Grates, made and Sold by SAMUEL EMMES, at his Shop on Ballard's Wharf, North End.

N. B. Anvil's faced and mended after the best Manner. Scotch and Louisbourg Coals Sold at the above Place.

Boston, December 1, 1768.

RAN-away from the Ship *John, Thomas Ashburne* Master, *five* indented Servants, named—*John Cotter, John Latind, Thomas Waterson, Edward Corlet* and *William Holmer,* each about Twenty Years old.—Whoever will take up any or the whole of said Servants, and bring them to said Thomas Ashburn, or John Rowe, at his Store, shall receive for each and every of said Servants, Three Dollars Reward—And all Captains of Vessels, and every other Person, are hereby strictly caution'd not to conceal or carry off any of the above-named Servants, as they will be strictly prosecuted for so doing, according to the Law made for that Purpose.

Best Sperma Ceti Candles,
Warranted Pure,

MADE AND SOLD by JOHN LANGDON in Fleet-Street, above HANCOCK's Wharf, near the *Old North Meeting House.* He also sells the best Refin'd Sperma Ceti Oil by the Barrel. Best *Tallow* Candles mould and dipp'd, and Bayberry Wax Candles. ALL as low as they can be had at any Place in Town.

William had had his ears cropped

Spruce beer in Boston at a dollar a barrel

New York to Baltimore in two days

Figs and Almonds.

100 Kegs fresh FIGS.
20 Bags soft-shell'd ALMONDS.
Just landed and to be sold on reasonable
Terms, by
William Seton, and Co.
New-York, Jan. 9, 1789.

For Falmouth,

The BRIG

BOON,

Thomas Orange Master,

Has excellent Accommodations for Passengers,
and will sail in about ten days, for Passage, only apply to the Captain on board, at Rosevelt's
Wharf, or to

RICHARD YATES,
No. 9, Princess-Street.
New-York, April 29, 1789.

London Porter.

THIS DAY WILL BE LANDED,
AT MURRAY'S WHARF,
From on board the Ship London, Capt. Woolsey,
56 Hogsheads Draught Porter,
For Sale by
WILLIAM SETON, and Co.
Who have on Hand,
500 Cases Florence Oil,
Of the latest Importation from Leghorn.
New-York, April 22, 1789.

Cricket Club.

THE Members of the CRICKET CLUB are
hereby notified, that the first Meeting for
the present Season, will be at the Old Ground, on
Thursday the 7th of May next. The Wickets to
be pitched at 3 o'clock.
Such Members who wish to propose any of their
Friends to fill the vacancies, occasioned by the re-
moval of some of the Members since the last Season, will please to return their names to the President as soon as possible.
New-York, April 20, 1789.

JAMES HAYS,

Leather Breeches Maker & Glover,
At the Sign of the *BUCK* and *BREECHES*,
No. 18, WATER-STREET, nearly opposite
the *Coffee-House*,
BEGS Leave to return his sincere Acknow-
ledgments to his Friends and the Public
in general, for the many Favors he has experienced and it shall be the Height of his Ambition to merit a Continuance thereof. From
his long Experience in Business in different
Parts of Europe, as well as in the capital Cities
of America, he flatters himself that he has it
in his Power to serve the Public as well as any
in America and those Gentlemen that please
to Favor him with their Commands, may depend on Punctuality and Dispatch and the least
Favors gratefully acknowledged, by
The Public's most humble Servant.
HE HAS FOR SALE,
A Complete New *Dutch Waggon.*
New-York, February 24, 1789.

WANTED,

AN Apprentice to the GOLD & SILVER-
SMITHS Business.——Enquire of the
Printer.

Leather breeches were indispensable in 1789

Paul Revere advertises his new retail shop

Potatoes were not common when Washington was president

In 1794 the well dressed man wore white silk stockings

went on quests of this sort with no qualms of conscience. At least one of them, who would not ordinarily sit at a table where liquor was served, spent weeks in "pubs" in English mill towns fishing for information from workmen for whom he bought drinks, or buying broken parts of machines in local repair shops. Sometimes by very questionable methods whole machines were secured, smuggled to France or Holland and shipped home by devious routes under false invoices. One American, who was fortunate enough to secure a complete textile machine in England, had it sawed in small pieces and shipped to France as plate glass. From there it was reshipped to America, where it was reassembled and many copies of it were made. These precautions were necessary to the success of the enterprise, for the British navy did not hesitate to overhaul ships on the high seas and take smuggled cargo back to England.

It was by these questionable methods that our infant industries had what must be referred to as an illegitimate birth. Whitney had invented the cotton gin which was soon feeding millions of pounds of cotton to the English mills, but it appeared that our inventive genius had stopped at the cotton patch. For several generations the only improvements we made in the production of cotton or any other kind of cloth came from the adoption of British machinery. In all of these nefarious thefts and smuggling enterprises the Yankee businessmen had the wholehearted support of our government officials who were stationed abroad. No one thought there was anything wrong about it except the British whose machines and trade secrets were being stolen.

The English had in an earlier day used exactly the same methods in picking up trade secrets from the more advanced manufacturers of the continent. Methods of slitting iron bars for nail-making were first perfected in Sweden where the secret was carefully guarded. The method was finally learned by a Stourbridge, England, blacksmith who was an accomplished amateur musician. He went to Sweden where he fiddled his way into the hearts of the workmen and returned home to set up a successful slitting mill.

The machine age dawned on the Americans so suddenly that they were somewhat dazzled. Machine production was so mystifying that it appeared to be possessed of some magical qualities. Many of the early capitalists seem to have assumed that once a machine, such as a spinning jenny or a power loom, was installed and the power applied, production would begin and the profits accumulate. It was only through costly experience that they learned that machines must be operated by trained men.

They then began to lean heavily on English technical experience, but with the naïve idea that any mill hand from Manchester, England, would be useful as manager, superintendent or foreman in any textile enterprise. The phenomenal reputation of Samuel Slater, whose success had aroused new ambitions, made every Manchester man a symbol of textile genius. Those who emigrated to the United States did not have to resort to very gross deception in order to secure jobs in the new textile enterprises which were springing up in many parts of the new country. Americans without technical experience who had failed to run the new machines didn't really know enough about textile manufacturing to tell an expert from an imposter.

One of these men was employed in a Massachusetts woolen mill to take care of the fulling and other processes connected with the finishing of rough woolen cloth to make it suitable for clothing. He insisted that he had gained knowledge of these mysterious processes at the cost of considerable time and money and he had a right to protect his secret knowledge from others. That was, at the time, considered to be a reasonable and natural attitude. Before production actually started everyone was afraid of overproduction. Owners were worried about their profits and workmen about their jobs.

The millowners readily agreed to provide this supposed expert with a private shop to which he alone had a key. Here he personally carried the rough unfinished woolens as they came from the looms. But as weeks went by nothing was brought out and he glibly explained this in technical terms the Yankee owners could not understand. At length they broke into the shop only to find that all of their product had been ruined by the inexpert handling of the supposed English expert.

There were quite a number of instances of this sort, probably all the result of the employment of men to do work for which they were technically unfitted. But the disgruntled Yankee millowners did not accept an explanation as simple as that. They were sure it was all a part of a plot to sabotage America's infant textile industry, instigated by the Manchester millowners and engineered by British consular officials in the United States. There may have been a certain amount of skullduggery and guerrilla trade warfare on the British side as well as ours. We were at this time making every effort, fair or foul—but mostly foul, to get models of textile machines out of England.

Textile mills of the early period did not, like those of today, carry out all the processes required to turn cotton and wool into cloth. Slater's mill, and many of those which followed his, did nothing more than produce yarn for weaving. The yarn was sold to women who wove their own cloth or sent out to homes to be woven for the account of the mill. Some of the woolen mills did nothing but shrink and otherwise prepare woolen homespun for the tailor. This process, in which nine yards of cloth would usually shrink to six, was the most difficult of all operations connected with the production of woolen cloth, and required not only machinery but expert workmanship.

The early industrialists had only a vague idea of the American factory system as it exists today, with men and women devoting their entire time and energies to factory work. Some of the manufacturing processes had to be carried out by machines at the mill, but it was the universal practice to have all possible handwork done in the home. Thus while the introduction of power spinning relieved the women on the farms of the work of spinning, it doubled or trebled the amount of weaving they did, for this became a standard method of bringing cash income to the farm home. Obviously only small establishments could be maintained by this spare time labor of the neighborhood. The proprietors of these early mills, like those of all other early industrial enterprises, were extremely reluctant to pay out any cash, partly because there was so little cash in circulation, and partly because they were ignorant of cost accounting and of factory management. The ideal arrangement toward which they all strove was to trade cloth for raw cotton, pay the mill employees in the same way, and give the home weavers a toll of the yarn they processed. If the proportions of exchange were properly worked out this would leave them with a satisfactory profit in the shape of surplus cloth which could be sold for cash.

About 1820 our textile industry came of age with the establishment of the great mills at Lowell, Massachusetts. Here for the first time the whole process of making cloth

from the raw cotton was completed by a single collection
of mills. In no other place in the world had this been done.
The enterprise was a large one which in a few years was
employing thousands of hands, mostly young women. The
transition from home to factory life was a sharp one, but
was mitigated by convent-like life of the mills. As there were
no streetcars or other means of transportation, it was necessary for the employees to be housed near their place of employment. This problem was solved by the erection of dozens
of company boarding houses and though the term "company
boarding house" later became significant of the exploitation
of labor, those at Lowell showed a consideration for the
health and comfort of the employees. The boarding houses
were not run at a profit. Each one was given rent free to a
"respectable woman" who was significantly known as a
"matron." The company paid her a fixed sum for the
board of the workers but the element of competition entered
into the arrangement, for each girl could board at any one
of the houses she liked.

The female employees were paid $1.75 per week and
board, the men seventy cents a day. All wages were paid in
cash. The amount of contemporary comment there was
about this would indicate that the arrangement was very
unusual. The hours of work appear to be long, but a Lowell
pastor in 1844 commented on them favorably. He pointed
out that in addition to Sundays there were four holidays a
year—Fast Day, July the Fourth, Thanksgiving and Christmas. Further consideration was shown by the fact that "no
lamps were lighted in the evening," implying that all work
ceased when it became too dark to see. He said that the girls
worked "an average of not more than ten and a half hours
a day." Accepting his figures as accurate, there were undoubt-

edly many summer days when the girls worked more than twelve hours.

No one found anything to criticize either in the hours of labor, the wage scale or the working conditions. In fact, Charles Dickens, who found little in America that deserved his praise, visited Lowell and wrote about the mills with some degree of enthusiasm.

Before the introduction of machinery and the construction of textile mills, clothing of all kinds was very expensive. It is difficult to make comparisons, but it is conservative to say that cloth of all kinds cost from three to five times present-day prices. Most of the locally made product was so coarse and imperfect that it would find no sale to clothing manufacturers today. Raw cotton, before the invention of the gin, sold for a dollar a pound. With Whitney's gins in operation the price dropped to thirty cents, a price that would make present day cotton farmers rich but boost the price of shirts. The cheapest and poorest cotton cloth, which would only be used for flour sacks today, sold for forty to sixty cents a yard. Perhaps it would not even be useful for that. A contemporary referred to cloth "so coarse that it could be punctured by a pea shooter." Broadcloth from which men's suits were made sold at five dollars a yard. It was from dark brown cloth of this sort made in Hartford, Connecticut, that Washington's first inaugural suit was tailored. The fact that the fastidious Washington was inaugurated in a suit wholly made in the United States was duly publicized and applauded. But the father of his country did not repeat the democratic gesture. At his second inauguration he was dressed in what was described as "a full suit of black velvet."

The cost of clothing dropped rapidly with the use of

machinery and continued to drop steadily as improved machinery was invented and perfected. As early as 1812 it was said that a workman using all of the improved textile machinery of the period could produce two hundred times as much cotton cloth in a given period as could have been produced by a single workman a few generations earlier. The well informed *Merchants Magazine* in 1844 commented on the steady reduction in the cost of cloth and said: "Shirtings, for example, which cost thirty years ago, sixty-two cents a yard, is now bought for eleven or twelve cents and equally good."

The Shakers, a communistic offshoot of the Quakers, came to America about the time of the Declaration of Independence. Their belief in the common ownership of property and community responsibilities made them successful manufacturers because religion supplied the discipline necessary to factory management. Having no incentive to work for individual profit, the Shakers shared their craft secrets with each other and so became the most skilled manufacturers in each of the few small communities in which they settled. They lived in huge community houses of fifty to a hundred rooms (males and females carefully separated) and worked on community farms and in community shops. Although the Congregationalists, the Episcopalians and the Evangelical sects, such as the Methodists and the Baptists, hated this heretical sect, they bought the Shaker furniture, brooms and woolen cloth. As one of the primary tenets of the Shakers was celibacy, it might have been presumed that the life of the sect would cover but a single generation. But a hundred years after the first Shakers came to America there were several thousand Shakers with few of them to be credited to converts.

Chapter III

THE ASSEMBLY LINE STARTS

In the summer of 1793 two young men living on a Georgia
plantation speculated on just how long it would be before
they would be millionaires—the first millionaires in the
United States. Every calculation brought them to the same
satisfactory conclusion. They would be very wealthy in only
a few years and, as far as they could see, they would continue
to pile up money for many years to come—more money than
they had ever dreamed of. The younger of the two men
was Eli Whitney, who would be twenty-eight near the end
of the year. The older man was Phineas Miller, who, like
Whitney, had attended Yale College. He had then come
south to act as plantation manager for Mrs. Nathaniel
Green, widow of the Revolutionary War hero and owner
of one of the largest plantations in the South. The estate
near Savannah had been given to Green by the state of
Georgia in recognition of his services in driving British
troops from the state.

Whitney had come south early that year looking for a
school-teaching job which did not develop, and was boarding
with the widow Green while looking for something to do.
School teaching wasn't the kind of work he was fitted for.
Books bored him and he had not been a very brilliant
student at New Haven. He liked to make things, to work with
hammers and saws and chisels, and he had a reputation of
being very clever with tools. When he was twelve years old
he had hammered out handmade nails which were said to

be just as good as those made by older men. While at Yale he had been a handy man for members of the faculty and did odd repair jobs for them. But it was beneath the dignity of a graduate of such a famous school to become a common mechanic—a Jack-of-all-trades. New England was full of good ones who could barely read and write. Education was on a plane far removed from practical things and graduates of colleges became either preachers, lawyers or teachers. It was a quarter of a century later before Yale began to teach such practical subjects as chemistry and geology.

The story of what Whitney did is familiar to every school boy. On the Green plantation he saw cotton plants for the first time and was impressed by the amount of hand labor required to pick a few pounds of lint from the cotton seeds. As a result, he invented a simple and inexpensive little contrivance that would separate ten times as much lint as could be picked by hand in the same period of time.

Never before had there been a merchandising opportunity of such dazzling possibilities. The needs of the whole world —then consisting of about a half billion people—contributed to the demand for this new machine. There were not enough shirts in the world, not enough clothing of any sort. It was easy enough to grow cotton, much easier than to grow flax or wool or silk. But the process by which the fluffy white balls could be turned into cloth was a long and tedious one. Indeed, with cotton linted, spun and woven by hand the total amount of labor involved in the construction of a shirt was about the same as that required to plow a corn field or get in the winter's supply of fire wood.

A start had been made in the production of cheaper clothing. Arkwright and Hargreaves had invented the spinning jenny and an improved loom, both originally used to make woolens and linens. Cotton cloth was something of a luxury, imported from India and China. The cost of picking the lint from the seeds was so great that cotton staple was more expensive than wool or flax. But Whitney and Miller knew that the gin would change this. In a long day's work a Negro slave could separate five pounds of lint from the seed. The one gin Whitney had made was small and crude, but with it fifty pounds of cotton could be linted in one day. With larger and better machines, possibly operated by mule power, they might lint more than a hundred pounds a day. Shirts for the millions were on the way! Future generations of poor as well as the rich could afford clothing that was neither ragged nor dirty! These were the things the two young New Englanders talked about, and the more they talked the greater grew the prospective fortune.

Most histories comment on the fact that Whitney never sold any of his machines. The truth of the matter is that he didn't intend to sell any of them. The plan he and Miller worked out was to set up their own gins in the cotton-growing areas and operate them like country grist mills, taking as toll one-third of the cotton linted. He had taken Miller into partnership in order to help finance the ambitious project. They had every reason to be confident that with the invention protected by a patent they would have a monopoly that would make them enormously wealthy. Every cotton grower, they felt sure, would be glad to bring his cotton to be ginned on that basis, for it was cheaper than hand-picking even when only slave labor was used. The profits from the operation of the gins were very easy to figure. One hand-operated machine would separate fifty pounds of lint a day. Cotton had never sold for less than twenty-five cents a pound so that the one-third share they took would be worth a little more than four dollars. In a week the cost of making the machine would be taken care of and the rest of the money could be put in the bank or used to manufacture and install more machines. A thousand of these small hand gins in operation meant four thousand dollars a day—more money than either of them had hoped to make in a year.

The two Yale men agreed that the gins should be manufactured in New Haven. There were more capable mechanics there than in Savannah, and these mechanics, knowing nothing about the growing of cotton, would probably be unable to guess what the strange contrivance was designed to do. They were going to take no unnecessary chances of the machine being copied. The original model was locked up in one of the plantation outbuildings. Full of hope for the future, Whitney returned to Connecticut and Miller remained in the South to buy or lease land for the location of the gins. Whitney was to return to Georgia as soon as he had made up a stock of machines and the matter of the patent rights had been finally settled. Then the money would begin to roll in.

Mrs. Greene talked. She took a good deal of credit to herself for the invention for she had been the first to suggest to her boarder that he see what he could do about making a machine to pull lint from the cotton seeds. She had seen the model gin in operation and couldn't resist the temptation to tell her neighbors something about this great invention. One night the building in which the model was stored was broken into and the model was stolen.

Clumsy imitations of the gin began appearing all through Georgia even before the patent rights were finally confirmed. Stories about this machine, which appeared to possess almost magical powers, spread throughout the South. It is difficult at this time to visualize the sensation it must have created—the wild and exaggerated tales that must have been told about it by the planters as well as by the ignorant and superstitious slaves. There were no machines of any kind in the South beyond the spinning wheel and the loom. Tools on the farm were of the most primitive sort. Everyone plowed with a wooden share on which scraps of metal were nailed. Not a wheel in the United States was turned by steam. All grain was reaped by hand sickles. Even such simple articles as pins and tacks were made by hand. The wooden parts of the gin were put together by hand-wrought nails and wooden pegs. Simple as it was, the cotton gin bridged several centuries at one leap. It must have been as amazing to the southern farmers as the radio would have been to us had it been presented as a practical instrument before the telephone or the phonograph.

The stolen model was copied and copies of that copy were copied. Any blacksmith could make a gin, and most of them in the South were soon busy filling orders placed by neighboring farmers. This was a clear violation of the inventor's patent rights but the violators were as hard to catch as the distillers of moonshine whiskey. They were probably more numerous than the latter, for there was at least one in every cotton-producing county. Even when one was caught redhanded, it was difficult to secure a conviction. No one knew much about this new-fangled idea of patent rights. The national government at Philadelphia was also new-fangled, and people were not certain how much attention should be paid to its laws. It was practically impossible to convince a southern jury that a blacksmith at the county seat had no right to make this urgently needed machine just because some damned Yankee had taken out a thing called a "patent." When Whitney and Miller tried to protect their rights by law suits, the matter became a political issue, raising the first sectional differences between the North and the South.

Miller spent all his money in the prosecution of law suits against infringers. Whitney neglected his factory to travel about in a vain attempt to secure justice and protect his rights. Cotton gins were bought everywhere but at the New Haven factory. So far as is known, Whitney and Miller never operated a single gin. Finally in desperation they tried to sell patent rights, but it was too late. No blacksmith would pay for the right to make a machine which every other blacksmith was making.

In the meantime the southern states were thriving. In 1784 eight bags of cotton (about four thousand pounds) landed at Liverpool and were seized by the customs for fraudulent entry on the ground that the southern states could not produce that amount of cotton. In 1791 the American production of cotton had amounted to 189,000 pounds. In 1801 exports had jumped to twenty-two million pounds and American business interests had become so great that an American Chamber of Commerce was established at Liverpool. Within three more years the exports had doubled and cotton still sold at about twenty-five cents a pound. If the two Yale men had been able to carry out their original plan for the ginning of all of the country's cotton, their toll would have been about fifteen million pounds—giving each of them a gross income of more than a million dollars for a single year. Robert Morris was the wealthiest man in the United States and he never possessed half that much money.

Some of the southern states recognized their moral obligations to the man who had brought the south undreamed prosperity. The legislature of South Carolina voted to pay Whitney fifty thousand dollars for the patent rights for the state, but he got only the first installment of twenty thousand dollars. There was probably little left after he had settled with the lawyers and the lobbyists who had pushed the measure through the legislature. North Carolina levied a license fee on each gin made in the state, which brought in about thirty thousand dollars. In the end Whitney was just as poor as he had been when he started. Miller, who had dreamed of such wealth, died impoverished. Plantation owners, real estate dealers, English cotton mills and several generations of slave traders all made money.

After five years of bitterly disappointing work, Whitney was through with cotton gins and with the South. Disgusted and disillusioned, he returned to New Haven and engaged in the manufacture of firearms. After his dreams of the great wealth which seemed to be securely in his grasp, he could not think of life as a school teacher. There were profits to be made from army contracts. The government was the only big and substantial customer in the country, the only organization requiring large supplies of any manufactured article. Whitney had not served the apprenticeship which would qualify him as a gunsmith. But while planning the manufacture of enough machines to gin all of the country's cotton he had evolved a new idea in manufacturing—an idea much more revolutionary and of more far-reaching importance than the invention of the gin.

As a matter of fact, if Whitney's only achievement had been the invention of the gin, he might quite justly have been set down as just a lucky young man, though not lucky enough to be rewarded. It is inconceivable that with so many Yankees puttering around with new mechanical devices much time would have elapsed before one of them had hit upon some device to pull the lint from cotton seeds. Whitney is certainly more deserving of undying fame because of his second contribution to the birth of the machine age. His gin revolutionized the agriculture of the South; but methods he introduced in the manufacture of firearms revolutionized the manufacturing processes of the world and pointed the course which led to our becoming the world's greatest manufacturing nation.

At the time Whitney built his musket factory, the method of making guns had not changed materially from the time that the first one was produced. Gunsmiths just took the material they needed and made a gun in the same way that carpenters made a piece of furniture, or tailors made a suit of clothes. Although thousands of guns might be made from the same model, no two guns were ever exactly the same unless by some almost impossible coincidence. There might be a slight difference in the length of the barrel or even in the size of the bore of different guns. The lock actuating the trigger which brought a piece of flint into contact with the steel and so set off the charge was the most important part of the mechanism. Yet no two triggers were exactly alike. Some pulled hard and some pulled soft. The thousands of guns used in the Revolutionary War were made in this way —one at a time.

Whitney had been thinking about manufacturing methods that would produce a very large number of machines at the least possible cost. The cotton gin was the first machine for which there was an immediate and very large demand, the first machine for which anything like mass production would be justified. The cotton business was finished, so far as he was concerned, but he knew his method of manufacture could be applied to other mechanisms composed of a number of closely related parts. So, although he was not a gunsmith and had never made a gun in his life, he went into the arms manufacturing business.

His plan was to make muskets with interchangeable parts. This meant that each part would be made with such precision that a trigger or any other part, could be taken from one musket and would work equally well in any other. It meant that parts would be made in wholesale quantities— not just one at a time—and then would be assembled to form a complete musket.

That has since become the standard practice in practically all manufacturing establishments, but in 1800 it was an entirely new idea and it is difficult at this time to realize how very revolutionary it was. All metal manufacturing was in the hands of artisans who, like the country blacksmiths, would make the complete article one at a time. If one part was a little larger or a little smaller than it should have been, the necessary adjustments were made. Gunsmiths had always had to do a little filing and bending and hammering to get the separate parts of a gun to fit, and it was inconceivable that guns could ever be made in any other way.

Whitney managed to convince the War Department that his plan was practical, and he got a contract for the manufacture of ten thousand rifles at $13.40 each. The cautious army officials made him put up a bond of thirty thousand dollars to be forfeited if he did not fulfill the contract. He was to deliver the whole ten thousand muskets in one year, which he failed to do. The manufacturing problem proved much more complicated than he had anticipated and as the work progressed he found greater and greater use for machines, drills and lathes and other metal working devices.

Most of these had to be constructed, for no machines like them had even been made before.

The delays were so great that the War Department would have been justified in cancelling the contract and demanding payment of the bond. When this point had been reached Whitney gave them a demonstration that was history-making in its significance. He took the parts of ten muskets to the War Department, laid them on a table and, choosing different parts at random, assembled ten perfect muskets —each one exactly like the others. It was as astounding as the wholly unexpected feat of a clever magician. The amazed officials not only gave him an extension of time on his contract but arranged financial help for him. He had to ask for many extensions. The contract was awarded March 7, 1799. He did not actually complete it until January 1, 1809, almost ten years later, just in time for the arms to be of service in the War of 1812.

Whitney's plan was brilliant, audacious and ambitious, and its execution demanded more planning and attention to detail than had ever before been undertaken by any manufacturer. The production of precision parts required the use of better tools than were then in existence and Whitney had not only to design them but to make them. At the end of the ten-year period he had in operation the first genuine arsenal ever built. Other so-called arsenals were just places where gunsmiths made guns. Whitney was doing more than just filling a contract for muskets. He was developing a system of production on which American industry of today is based.

The first assembly line in the world was in operation just as we were beginning to make the goods we had previously bought from England. With the manufacture of that lot of muskets by a new and revolutionary method, American manufacturing started on its way with a speed that has never slackened. Many new problems had to be solved, many new techniques perfected, an entirely new relationship between employers and workmen established. The net result was the production of goods of constantly improving quality at constantly decreasing cost.

The work of no other man has had such a profound effect on the lives of his fellow man. The cotton gin had changed the living habits of the civilized world. Days of hand labor had been necessary for the production of the most simple garment. Only the very rich were decently dressed. Soon all over the world in such far away places as India, Egypt, Brazil and China crude imitations of Whitney's gin were at work cutting in half the cost of cotton clothing. Millions of people who had never been able to buy a shirt could afford them now. The owners of cotton fields prospered because there was a wider market for the product. The manufacture of muskets with standardized and interchangeable parts marked the beginning of a revolution of equal importance in a much wider field. While the cotton gin fastened slavery on the South for generations, Whitney's new process of manufacturing dealt a death blow to another form of human slavery —the apprenticeship system—before it had an opportunity to become well established in the new country.

Before this time every piece of merchandise from the most simple to the most complicated had been made under the apprentice and artisan system. The apprentice in any trade—and there were dozens—was required to serve a long period during which he was a kind of wage slave to his master. He did not gain his complete personal freedom until the end of his period of apprenticeship—seven to twelve years. The laws regarding slaves and apprentices were practical identical. Employers in New York and New England advertised rewards for the return of runaway apprentices just as southern cotton growers advertised for runaway slaves. In England, where the apprentice system reached its highest development, its evils were so great that they were the subject of legislation over a period of several centuries.

Because of the methods used in producing the ten thousand muskets at Whitney's New Haven factory, it was not necessary to employ gunsmiths exclusively. There were many simple parts that could be made by a blacksmith. The wooden stocks could be made by a carpenter. Some parts required great precision in manufacture, others considerable manual strength. There was useful work for the unskilled as well as for those of varying degrees of skill. His factory, conducted on this new plan, provided immediate employment for young men who, under the old system, would have been compelled to spend years in a profitless apprenticeship before they could begin to work for themselves. No doubt there were grumbling and prophecies of failure on the part of the old-fashioned gunsmiths. But with a contract for ten thousands muskets there was work for all, and the gunsmiths attained a new dignity as superintendents and foremen in charge of various operations.

Whitney's plan worked even more successfully than he had anticipated. By dividing the work into different categories of skill he was able to employ a great many men at a wage much less than that paid to the master gunsmiths. But that was neither the only nor the most important saving in operation. As each workman was concerned only with the production of one part, each soon developed a highly specialized skill.

Most of all, this American system of manufacturing which was universally adopted was of great benefit to the consumer —to the customers who were later to buy the never ending and always increasing products of American factories. Whitney, who failed in attempts to sell the first products of his own genius, laid the foundations for the growth of the great merchandising organizations that were to follow. The mass production of the assembly line meant the production of cheaper and better merchandise of standard quality. By the employment of workmen of varying degrees of skill he spread employment over a wider range and so created more customers for the products of the American factories which were to follow.

Chapter IV

MERCHANDISE FOR THE MASSES

AT THE time of the Boston Tea Party there were only a few hundred clocks in the thirteen colonies. There was no particular need for them—no trains to catch, and boats sailed with the tide. No wages were on an hourly basis and the work day was generally from sunrise to sunset. A few of the well-to-do people had sundials—others could tell when it was noon by noting when the shadow of a stake or of the corner of a house fell on a certain spot. That was accurate enough for all practical purposes. Of course these devices were useless on cloudy days and when the sun had set, but soon after dark everyone was supposed to be in bed. There were more hour glasses than clocks, mostly used to time cooking operations. No one counted time very accurately. Only a half century before this the best clocks in Europe, most of them owned by kings and princes, had only hour hands. The only place where a clock was really needed in church-going communities was in the meeting house. Evening services could be set for "early candle lighting" but no natural device of this sort could be used to determine the time to ring the bell for the morning service.

The result of this was that our early clockmakers were dependent almost entirely on the church trade, were intimate with the ministers, and curried favor with church leaders who might have a voice in awarding a contract. A clockmaker who was not a churchgoer had a hard time making a living. But if he could land one church contract a year, he was secure and well on the way to making a fortune. Next of importance was the making of the tall "grandfather" clocks which distinguished the homes of the wealthy Americans. After Whitney's success with the musket contract, American clockmakers turned from these highly specialized and narrowly restricted markets and became the first producers of merchandise for the masses. Appropriately enough the story of how this was done begins with the Boston Tea Party, or the events leading up to it.

Thomas Harland, a passenger on the ship which brought the provocative cargo of China tea to Boston, was a London clockmaker who had decided to practice his trade in the colonies. He had made his arrangements beforehand, had brought his tools and materials with him, and was ready to set up shop at once. Even before Paul Revere and the other Boston boys had painted their faces like Indians and thrown the 340 chests of tea to the codfish, Harland had rented a shop in Norwich, Connecticut, and placed an advertisement in the Norwich *Packet*. In the issue of December 9, 1773, he begged "leave to acquaint the public that he had opened a shop near the store of Christopher Leffingwell." Here he offered to make all kinds of clocks and watches, "neat as in London and at the same price." He must have prospered, for six years later he built a house which still stands as one of the historical show places of Norwich.

Following the custom of the period, he took on a great many apprentices who worked for him for seven years for little more than board and keep. Clockmaking was a new occupation and ambitious boys wanted to learn it just as boys of today want to learn radio or aeronautical engineering. Unlike other trades, such as carpentry or blacksmithing, a man could work at clockmaking after age had robbed him of the strength of his arms. One of Harland's apprentices was Eli Terry who started work in the clock shop at the age of fourteen.

At the end of seven years Terry had mastered the trade and set up in business for himself. He must have acquired a reputation for skill while he was still an apprentice, for he did not have to wait long for his first order, which came from a church. Other orders followed and he built a number of church clocks which are still ticking away after more than a century and a half. No doubt he could have continued for years in this highly respectable branch of the business. But other clockmakers had arrived from London, other boys had served their time as apprentices, and it was easy to foresee a time when there would be a clock in every steeple—unless the parishioners were too poor to afford one. Terry filled a few orders for clocks for individuals and then made the bold decision to go into clockmaking on a wholesale basis. In order to appreciate the courageousness of this decision, it is necessary to understand the way in which the needs of customers were satisfied at this time.

There was no such thing as a clock shop where timepieces could be bought out of stock. Each clock was made to order. In fact, at this period the manufactured articles that could be bought in shops were very limited. If a man wanted a pair of shoes, a carriage, a chair or a clock, he went to the appropriate shop and ordered it made. The idea that an artisan should invest labor and material in the manufacture of an article in the faith that some one might drop in and buy it had not yet developed.

Terry planned activities too extensive for a small shop and started what was doubtless the first clock factory in the world. In 1803 he bought an old mill at Plymouth, Connecticut, and began making clocks for which customers were yet to be found. The factory was probably nothing more than a large room where the benches of the workmen and the apprentices were placed and the lumber stored. Terry made the master clock, or model, himself and the workmen copied it, each man working on an individual clock. That had been the standard procedure in all clock shops. With the exception of the escape wheel, which was of brass, the weights of iron and the bushings of ivory, all the other parts of the clock were of wood which the workmen cut from the forests about them. The movements were of beech, maple or sycamore, the wheels of cherry, pear or apple.

When four clocks had been completed, Terry packed them on a horse and traveled to neighboring farms and villages to sell them. One clock was packed in each saddlebag, one behind the saddle and one in front. There was no room for the rider until the return journey was begun after the clocks had been sold. The clocks cost about twenty-five dollars each, which was a great deal of money and he had to sell them on the installment plan, because very few people could afford to pay out that much cash at one time. In fact, very few clocks were bought for cash. Terry needed food for his family and his workmen, and salt pork or corn meal was just as useful as money. Or payment could be made in woven cloth or handmade iron nails, beeswax, cheese or any other useful commodity. He sold or bartered some of these articles on his return journey.

Terry was one of the first men in the world to engage in manufacturing and merchandising in the modern sense of the word—that is, he produced an article that was a convenience rather than a necessity—something that had to be sold. That was not true of the new American textile mills, which were spinning and weaving a very small amount of woolen cloth and a still smaller amount of cotton. People had to have cloth but they could do without clocks. The Yankee peddler was a well-known institution before Terry was born, but he sold tinware, needles, thread, and buttons—articles that were household necessities. Terry initiated the plan of installment selling and also the other sales stratagem of leaving his clocks on free trial. The two selling aids went together. A clock was a strange object to most of the potential customers. They did not know whether or not it would continue to run and, even if it did run, whether or not it would keep time with enough accuracy to be of any practical benefit.

So Terry adopted the practice of leaving the clocks in homes, promising to pick them up on his return journey if the householders decided they did not want to buy. He had to take back very few, for after the prospective customer had seen the pendulum swinging and heard the clock ticking for a few weeks he was in no mood to part with it. Clocks dominated the room then to a much greater degree than they do now, for they were sold without cases and known as "wag on the wall." On subsequent visits Terry made adjustments and collected installments until the clock had been paid for.

As soon as he had accumulated enough working capital in the form of a winter's supply of provisions for his family and workmen, he adopted a plan of seasonal manufacture and selling. Before this he had been compelled to dispose of the clocks as fast as they were produced, which meant braving the discomforts of New England winters to search for customers. With a prosperous business and a growing volume he was able to abandon this system. Now he and his workmen remained in his little mill all winter and by the time pleasant spring weather came they might have as many as a hundred clocks to dispose of. He and his workmen, who were also salesmen, then used more pack horses, carried a larger consignment of cargo and traveled farther afield, selling clocks as far north as Boston and as far south as New York.

Often Terry found that the reputation of his clocks had preceded him, that people would buy a Terry clock because they knew it would run and keep time accurately. With this consumer acceptance of his product he was able to turn the selling over to others and devote his time to the factory. He had other ambitious plans in mind. As he had traveled about, Terry had been impressed by the great number of people who wanted a clock but could not afford to buy one at a price of twenty-five dollars, although that was about the lowest price at which a clock had ever been sold. He worked continually and successfully to lower costs of manufacture and succeeded in producing a clock which sold for twelve dollars, but still he was not satisfied.

Whitney, who was working at New Haven only thirty miles away, had proved that muskets could be made successfully by producing standardized and interchangeable parts, and Terry decided to adopt the same method of production in his growing factory. His ambition was to produce a clock that could be sold for five dollars. That did not mean that a clock could be placed in every home, for the weekly wage of a skilled workman was only two dollars and fifty cents, so that a five dollar clock represented the wages for two weeks of work. But a five dollar clock as a piece of merchandise that had never been dreamed of. He felt sure it would mean production measured in hundreds instead of dozens.

As soon as he proved to himself that clocks could be made

in this way, he bought a larger mill and installed some machinery. Then he made the sensational announcement that he was placing in production and would make in one continuous operation no less than five hundred clocks all of the same design. Nothing like this had ever been attempted. Whitney, of course, had started on the bold enterprise of producing ten thousand muskets but the government had contracted to buy the muskets before a wheel was turned. Terry had to sell his merchandise after he made it. A few years ago when we were still getting thrills from the motor car, there were gasps of astonishment when Detroit manufacturers announced plans to turn out in a single season a few thousand cars. No announcement of that sort was so sensational as this one made by Terry in 1807. Many of his competitors in a lifetime of work had never produced five hundred clocks. There were doubtless a good many predictions that if Terry did succeed in his mad scheme most of the clocks would gather cobwebs in his shop, for it was inconceivable that there could be that many people who would buy them. Terry was not a philanthropist and was inspired by no idealistic urge to make life better for his fellow man. Like many later manufacturers who followed his methods and duplicated his success, he was just a hardheaded and very practical business man who saw that there was money to be made by producing an article that could be sold at a lower unit price and so reach a greater number of customers.

He not only made and sold the first five hundred clocks but started production on another lot. He followed Whitney's method of having each workman make a single part and wherever possible introduced the use of machinery. At the end of three years he had made and sold no less than five thousand clocks. His was the only factory in the world making a clock that the man who was only moderately well-to-do could afford to buy. But the assembly line process of manufacture had been applied to the production of merchandise for the millions, and there was steady progress from that time to this when the poorest paid laborer can, in less than two hours of work, earn enough money to buy a clock —a better clock than Terry made.

By the time Terry got through with his ambitious plan we were very probably better supplied with clocks than any other nation in the world. He and his successors continued to make an increasing number of clocks and at constantly decreasing prices. In the old world the making of clocks was in the hands of jewelers who catered to what might be called the "palace trade." A timepiece was considered a regal gift— was what Henry VIII gave to the unfortunate Anne Boleyn as a wedding present. For half a century the development of the business in the old and new world followed opposite lines. The old world craftsmen sought for improvements in design and decoration that would justify charging a higher price and so earn a greater profit on the individual item. Museums are full of these old timepieces covered with gilt and useless gadgets. The American manufacturers, on the other hand, constantly tried to simplify the design so that the individual item could be sold at a smaller price and so reach a larger number of customers. That was the aim of Eli Terry as it has been the consistent aim of American manufacturers who have succeeded him.

By the time Americans had learned how to roll brass and could stamp clock parts out of that easily worked metal, the Connecticut clockmakers were ready to go into the export business. Chauncey Jerome was the pioneer in the export of clocks, the first American manufacturer to sell his product abroad in any substantial volume. And no manufacturer before or since captured a foreign market so easily and with such negligible selling cost. Jerome prepared to sell his clocks in England the same way that they had been sold at home—by sending a shipment to London accompanied by a salesman. The name of the salesman was Epaphroditus Peck, a member of the Connecticut family which has been famous for generations for the jaw-breaking names bestowed on its sons. When Mr. Peck produced the invoice for the shipment of clocks, the British customs authorities denounced Jerome as a fraud, insisting that clocks could not under any circumstances be produced at such a cheap price. Manufacturers in Holland were selling some cheap clocks in England, but their prices were far above these on the American's invoice. To the official mind it was obvious that the clever Yankee clockmaker had made out a fraudulent invoice so as to escape payment of the full customs duty.

The British law had devised a simple but effective penalty for frauds of this sort. The law provided that the goods could be seized by the government which would pay the importer the invoice price plus ten per cent and not a single farthing more. That would make him the victim of his own trick and teach him not to try to defraud the British government!

That was what was done and without doing any work or attempting to contact a single customer, Mr. Peck was given a treasury draft for an amount representing a satisfactory profit on the entire shipment of clocks. The clocks had been honestly invoiced and to sell them all in one lot, and for cash, with no trouble and expense was something in the nature of a merchandising miracle the like of which had never occurred before.

But it did occur again with the same actors, the same stage

settings and the same scenery. The jubilant Mr. Peck forwarded the money to his boss in Bristol, Connecticut, and settled comfortably in London to await the arrival of more clocks. As soon as Jerome heard about the fortunate turn of events in England he put on extra men in his own factory, bought complete clocks of standardized and easily assembled parts from other manufacturers and rushed another shipment. The astute Mr. Peck may have managed it so that this shipment would come to the attention of a new set of British customs officials. In any event, they took the same action as was taken by the first lot of officials, compulsory sale and prompt payment by the British treasury. Mr. Peck went back to his comfortable lodgings in London, which he was beginning to like very much.

It was not until the third shipment of cheap Connecticut clocks had arrived that the officials awoke to the fact that all that Jerome had been trying to do was to sell his clocks and that his invoices had been honest. After that his shipments were accepted in the usual way and duty collected on the invoice valuation. In the meantime the Jerome clocks had been sold at what appeared to be sacrifice prices by the British treasury and the Jerome trade-mark was well established. When shipments began coming through in the regular way Mr. Epaphroditus Peck had no difficulty about sales. He remained in London a prosperous and successful business man until his death.

Having by his mass production methods produced a clock that was both cheap and serviceable, Terry next turned his attention to the manufacture of a clock that would be more convenient and more ornamental. All of the clocks he had made had been of the grandfather variety. The wooden works did not occupy a great amount of space but the pendulum was long and there had to be plenty of room for the weights to drop. The only place for a clock of this sort was on the wall. His clocks were sold without cases which the owner could have made by a cabinetmaker. Many preferred to leave the caseless clock hanging on the wall where they could see the pendulum swinging to and fro and so be conscious of the fact that the clock was running. Terry's next contribution was a shelf clock—an instrument that could be placed on the mantel—an ornament as well as a timekeeper. With this he designed a distinctive case which he called "Pillar Scroll Top Case." He proposed to sell clock and case as a single unit—something that had never been done before in America. British manufacturers had been making handsome and expensive clocks of this type, but they had the advantage of being able to use springs. We had no steel good enough to make clock springs and the British would sell us none. All our early manufacturers had to use weights.

In the meantime Seth Thomas had gone into the clock business, first as an employee and later as a partner of Terry's. The partnership had been dissolved and at this time, 1810, Thomas was in business for himself. He knew that there was a future in the clock business, believed that the new design his old employer had worked out would have a larger sale than anything that had been produced before. He paid Terry no less than one thousand dollars for the privilege of making this new clock, a very large sum for that time. The patent rights do not appear to have been sold on a royalty basis. Thomas paid the thousand dollars outright and secured the privilege of making as many clocks as he liked. It was a bold venture but successful, for the Seth Thomas organization has continued in uninterrupted operation from that day to this, a period of more than a hundred and thirty years. In the first year Thomas made six thousand clocks and Terry an equal number. The following year the Thomas factory produced ten thousand clocks and every year since then the production has increased until now it is more than ten thousand clocks an hour.

Terry and Thomas and many other pioneers made the first of the many contributions that our manufacturers have made toward the democratic American way of life—possibly a greater contribution than that of the statesmen who have so eloquently expounded it. His successful manufacture of cheap clocks had a great deal of social significance. A good many years were to elapse before, with a rising scale of wages and decreasing costs of production, a clock would be made so cheaply that the poorest could possess one. But the reduction in price from twenty-five to five dollars greatly broadened the range of those who could afford a clock—decreased the number of have-nots. That is a process that has been going on continuously.

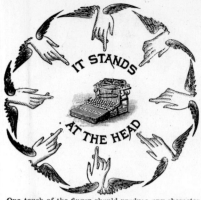

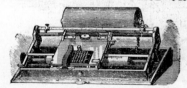

Pioneer typewriter manufacturers were not modest

Hideous things were made from lace flax threads

MACKEY'S
RAILROAD AND STEAMBOAT GUIDES.

ALWAYS RELIABLE.

**MACKEY'S OFFICE DIRECTORY.   MACKEY'S INDICATOR.
MACKEY'S A. B. C.   MACKEY'S EXPRESS GUIDE.**

Getter up of Time Tables for Advertisers.
ADDRESS
JOSEPH MACKEY, 88 White Street, New York.
MY GUIDES ARE TO BE SEEN EVERYWHERE.   7.26

Mr. Hagan's wonderful preparation brought beauty to all

BRANDY, BRANDY, BRANDY.

Now landing 1,000 gallons superior Cognac Brandy. For Sale low, at the
37-tf   BEE HIVE.

WM. S. CLARK,

STORAGE, FORWARDING, AND COMMISSION MERCHANT AND GENERAL AUCTIONEER.

Respectfully informs the public that he has permanently located in the Town of San Francisco, for the purpose of conducting all the various branches connected with a GENERAL COMMISSION business.

AUCTION SALES of every description attended to in any part of the Town or District.

☞ WARE-HOUSE and Office at the Stone Pier foot of Broadway.   19-6m*

WINE & AGUADIENTE.

Just landed ex Brig "Malek Adhel" seventy barrels Wine and Aguadiente, for Sale low, at the
37-tf   BEE HIVE.

PASTURAGE.

The Subscriber will receive at his Rancho situated three miles from Mission San Francisco de Dolores, horses or cattle to pasture throughout the year. Grazing good at all seasons. Terms reasonable. Animals received upon the grounds, and there retained until demanded. No risk to be assumed by the grazier.
                    ROBT. T. RIDLEY.
San Francisco, Dec. 17th, 1847.   32-tf

NAILS, NAILS, NAILS.

100 kegs superior Fall River Cut Nails, in lots to suit purchasers, at the
37-tf   BEE HIVE.

TEA, TEA, TEA.

400 boxes Green & Black Tea just landed ex "Lady Adams" and "Anita" to be sold low, in quantities to suit the trade. This article can confidently be recommended as a most superior article at the
                          BEE HIVE,
37   San Francisco.

HOUSE AND SIGN PAINTING.
BY
T. W PERRY.

All jobs intrusted to him will be done in a workman like manner and on reasonable terms. For further information apply at the store of C. L. Ross, or at the dwelling house of Mr. MERILL
San Francisco, Nov. 10. 1847   26-6m

NEW FERRY HOUSE AT BENICIA.

The subscriber is now building a house on the opposite side of the Straits for the comfort and accommodation of persons wishing to pass from the south side. He intends hereafter to keep a boat on each side, that persons will not be detained a moment longer that the tide and weather requires. He has, and will keep on hand, barley and corn for horse feed.
                          R. SEMPLE,
                              Proprietor.
Benicia City, Sept. 1847.   22-y

PUBLIC HOUSE.

PETER DAVIDSON, begs leave to inform his friends and the public that he has opened a House at the "Pueblo de San Jose." His table will be constantly supplied with the best the country affords; his rooms are large, airy and commodious; at his Bar will be found the choicest liquors and wines.

N. B.—Oyster suppers supplied at short notice.   27-tf

L. W. HASTINGS.
Attorney and Counsellor at Law, and Solicitor in Chancery :

Will now devote his entire attention to his profession; he will attend to the collection of debts, and to all other business connected with his profession, in any portion of the Territory ; he will also attend to the collection of foreign debts, either in the Sandwich Islands, Oregon, or any portion of the United States, and to the collection of debts and the remission of money due to foreign creditors.

All professional business intrusted to his care will receive his prompt and assiduous attention.

Office in San Francisco, U. C.   32-tf

WHO WOULDN'T WEAR SOCKS.

When they can be had at the Bee Hive at half the usual prices.   28-tf

TAILORING. -

The Subscriber will make all kinds of citizens Clothing in the most approved style.— Also, Military Clothing according to Law and with elegance. Will also, teach the science and art of cutting, to new beginners.

LAAGGGOONN, San Francisco, Montgomery Street
37-y   LAZARUS EVERHART.

IRON-MONGERY & CARPENTERS TOOLS just landed.

1 case assorted Iron Mongery, low for cash at the
37-tf   BEE HIVE

FERRY AT BENICIA CITY.

Persons wishing to pass the Bay of SAN FRANCISCO will hereafter find a good substantial FERRY BOAT at the Straits of Carquinez

There is a good level road from the Mission of Santa Clara by the Mission of San José and Amador's Ranch, distance fifty miles; from Benicia City to Sonoma 25 miles; from Benicia City to New Helvetia fifty miles. It will be perceived that this is the nearest, and much the best road from Santa Clara to New Helvetia, and from Santa Cruz to Bodega.

RATES OF FERRIAGE

For crossing, a man and horse, $1 00
" horses, each,   1 00
    footman,   0 50
            R. SEMPLE, Proprietor.

FERRY AT MONTEZUMA.

An excellent Ferry Boat is now in full operation at Montezuma, sufficiently large to cross twenty head of horses or horned cattle. Persons crossing at Montezuma will find an excellent waggon road from that place to the Pueblo de San Jose, Monterey, Suisuin, Nappa, Sonoma, New Helvetia and all the Sacramento Valley.

Distance from Montezuma to Suisuin, 15 miles, to Nappa, 30 miles, to Sonoma, 40 miles, to Knight's and Gordon's settlement, 30 miles, to New Helvetia, 35 miles, to the Pueblo de San Jose, 50 miles, and to Monterey, 120 miles

RATES OF FERRIAGE.

For crossing each head of horses, $0 50
"   "   "   " horned cattle,   50
"   "   "   footman,   50
"   "   " wagon, $3 00
            J. LAIRD,
40-tf   Proprietor.

San Francisco's first furniture factory was established in 1847

The "Tablette" Lamp,

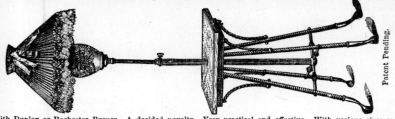

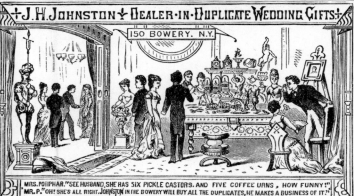

Mr. Johnston was a friend of all brides

Chapter V

JOHN FITCH AND HIS APPRENTICESHIP

THE story of the experiences of the unfortunate John Fitch when he was apprenticed to the Cheney brothers is worth telling for the reason that it illustrates the evils of a system we escaped because we began our manufacturing with the use of machinery. During the centuries before this, when all merchandise was produced by hand labor, the master of a shop depended on the unpaid labor of apprentices, and it was inconceivable that a shop could be run in any other way. The lad usually began his apprenticeship at the age of fourteen. For seven years he was the legal property of his master who was theoretically obligated to feed and clothe him and teach him his trade. At the end of that period the boy would be of age—the master of a trade and privileged to set up in business for himself or to go to work for wages. The usual terms provided that at the end of the period he would be given a suit of clothing and sometimes a small amount of cash.

Sometimes the agreement was for a longer term. One Salem, Massachusetts, youth was apprenticed to a goldsmith for a period of twelve years with the stipulation that he would be paid fifteen dollars at the end of that period. Apprenticeship agreements were looked on as being of considerable value to the master of the shop. When apprentices ran away, as they often did, their masters advertised, offered rewards for their apprehension and they were treated in the same way as runaway slaves. When a master died or went bankrupt, the unexpired time of his apprentices was listed among his assets to be bought by anyone who cared to pay the asking price. Sometimes solvent masters sold the unexpired time of their apprentices, which was an easy and convenient method of raising money. The relation was not that of employer and employee but of master and servant, the latter being completely under the control of the former. It was a system under which the apprentice was as defenseless as the slave, but its injustices were endured because it was the only way a boy could learn a trade. By enduring seven years of servitude he could escape a lifetime of work as a farm hand or a common laborer.

The prohibition and restriction of manufacturers in the colonies had prevented the growth of the apprenticeship system here and the introduction of the machine method of manufacturing coincided with the beginning of our industries. It was never more than a rather unimportant episode in our history, serving now as an historical landmark to show us what we escaped. Our workmen from the beginning were free and independent wage earners while those of other countries still are handicapped by the tradition of apprenticeship. There are but faint traces of the system to be found in some of our trades and industries.

While the apprenticeship experiences of John Fitch, the inventor of the steamboat, were unusual, they illustrate very graphically the cruel way in which the whole system could be exploited by unscrupulous masters at the expense of poor boys who were willing to make sacrifices in order to learn a trade. John, the son of an impoverished farmer, was about seventeen years old when Benjamin Cheney, a well-known Connecticut clock master, offered to take him into his shop. The terms offered were far from liberal, but the boy was willing to accept them because of all the trades in New England that of clockmaker was considered the best. John was enthusiastic about the opportunity but met with no encouragement from his father, who was having a hard time making a living on a worn-out farm and who wanted the son to remain at home until he was twenty-one years old to help with the farm work.

The elder Fitch was one of many New England farmers who made the most of the fact that they had property rights over their children until they came of age. Timothy King, a local weaver, had fallen in love with Sarah Fitch but the girl's father held out against the marriage because she was only sixteen years old and therefore he could profit by two more years of her work. He offered consent to the marriage only if the lovesick young man would agree to weave all the clothing for the Fitch family during the two remaining years of his wife's minority. The young people showed a good deal of independence for that period, for they defied convention, got married without parental consent and, according to all accounts, lived happily.

The usual procedure was for a father to arrange for the apprenticeship of his son. Sometimes he used this as a method of shifting to another the responsibility for supporting and disciplining an unruly son. Apprenticeship was also a convenient method of taking care of orphans without cost to the public. When a poor boy was "on the town," it was the custom of the authorities to apprentice him as soon as possible. This usually meant that the unfortunate youngster had to slave for his master until he was of age and got nothing in return but his keep and possibly a new suit of clothes. Frequently he learned nothing but how to pitch hay, cut firewood, curry horses and milk cows. Sometimes the terms of the indenture provided the father with some actual cash, for sons were apprenticed under the same terms that the labor of slaves might be rented. In other cases, affectionate fathers made a careful investigation of the masters and saw to it that their sons were well treated. John's father did nothing. The boy had to make his own arrangements in the hope of getting parental approval.

Negotiations with Benjamin Cheney over the terms were long drawn out and difficult. John did his best to protect himself and make sure that he accomplished his one ambition, which was to learn the clockmaker's trade. He knew that a great many other boys had been apprenticed to learn some trade or other and then had spent the whole term working on their master's farms or doing manual labor. At a much later date, Millard Fillmore, one of the half-forgotten presidents of the United States, was treated in this manner. He was apprenticed to a fuller, who taught him nothing about the processing of woolen cloth but kept him busy cutting firewood and tending fires. It was taken for granted that some work of this sort should be done, for almost every artisan had his small farm and all hands pitched in at the planting and harvest season. But some masters kept their apprentices busy all the time at work of this sort—using them as farm hired hands without pay. Young Fitch tried to protect himself from a fate of this kind by an agreement making a fair apportionment of his time. The contract which he negotiated provided that during the term of his apprenticeship, that is until he was twenty-one years old, he would work seven months of each year at his trade and five months at "chores" or outdoor work. During the entire period he would receive no wages.

Cheney finally agreed to this, but the elder Fitch made

objections. He would need help himself at harvest time and he insisted that John work on his farm three weeks of each year. John had to thresh this out with Cheney, taking care to see that the three weeks be taken out of the five months which he was supposed to spend at chores rather than the seven months of each year when he hoped to be working at his trade. Cheney finally agreed to that but, to offset this concession, insisted that the boy provide his own "cloathes." The elder Fitch might have given in on this point but the boy's stepmother was dead set against it. One of the reasons she had married the widower was that he had some useful children and now they were slipping away from her. Sarah should have been at home doing most of the housework instead of setting up housekeeping on her own.

As a last resort young Fitch appealed to his brother-in-law, Sarah's husband, and the latter agreed to provide him with clothing on credit. Timothy said:

"John, go ahead and learn that trade and I will find you in clothes and pay me when you can."

John had expected to pay dearly for the privilege of learning a trade and, harsh as the terms were, he was satisfied and as happy as an undernourished, sickly boy could be expected to be. But he had no conception of the difficulties and humiliations which would beset him as soon as he moved into the clockmaker's home. Mrs. Cheney did not uphold the Puritan traditions. She drank quantities of cheap rum and got drunk and when drunk she got sick, and John had to clean up after her. She couldn't keep a maid. She paid little attention to housework and he had to wash the dishes. She spent as little time as possible cooking. Once in an unusual burst of energy she filled a huge pot with salt mutton and beans and cooked up a mess which was pretty satisfactory —especially as there was a lot of it. But that was all the boy had to eat for almost a fortnight. When he complained that it was too salty, his mistress just put more water in the pot. At the end of twelve days what was left was so rancid that no one could eat it, and it was fed to the pigs.

The apprenticeship agreements usually placed on the master the responsibility for the religious instruction of the apprentice. In fact, religious prejudice had its place in the usual agreements. It was rare for a father to apprentice his son to a master of a denomination other than his own, as that would mean that the boy might be weaned away from the true faith. The Methodist father considered it better to indenture his son to a cruel skinflint of a fellow Methodist than to a liberal and kindly Congregationalist. Better for the boy to endure indignities and cruelties for seven years than to suffer the torturing fires of hell throughout eternity. The Congregationalist thought the same way about it, perhaps even more strongly. Father Fitch was such an uncompromising fundamentalist that he would not allow his children to pick up a fallen apple on Sunday, but for some reason he allowed his son to attach himself to a family where there would not only be no "religious instruction" but the environment was scandalously unwholesome.

As Benjamin Cheney had lived forty years without marrying, he was looked on as a confirmed old bachelor, a queer egg whom a woman would marry only for his wealth, and then very reluctantly. Even in his youth he was not calculated to palpitate maidenly hearts. In his babyhood he had suffered from rickets and other infantile diseases with the result that his head was monstrous and ill-shapen, about twice the size of the normal head. Monstrosities like this were much more common in colonial New England than at present, but women avoided Benjamin.

Men did not avoid the future Mrs. Cheney nor did she avoid them, but she never got them to the point where they would marry her. She was the sister of Timothy Cheney's wife and Timothy was Benjamin's brother. With sullied spinsterhood facing her she adopted a rather bold strategy to attract the attention of the only man in the neighborhood who might consciously lead her to the altar. Her position was rather desperate, for being neither maid, wife nor widow she did not fit into any of the conventional niches of outwardly respectable Connecticut. On one of Benjamin's prolonged visits to his brother Timothy she, as a playful gesture, slipped into his bed and he found her there when he undressed in the dark and went to bed. The romance started in this unconventional way resulted in marriage. At the time John began his apprenticeship they had, as he said in his copious autobiography, "managed to scramble up a lively son who was about two years old." As the drunken mistress was frequently incapacitated and without a maid, John, who was burning to become a clockmaker, frequently had to clean the baby and change his diapers.

The weeks passed filled with work of chopping wood, building fires, washing dishes and taking care of the baby but without John ever getting more than a passing glimpse of the shop which enshrined the mysteries of the craft he wanted to learn. In order to make sure that he would be given a fair deal, he began keeping a journal, setting down the hours he spent in doing chores. Against this he intended to set up another column of figures crediting his master with the time spent in the shop learning his trade. The total of hours spent at chores mounted rapidly. He had to be up before anyone else in the household stirred and was usually the last to go to bed. Frequently he spent sixteen hours of the day at dishwashing, baby tending, cow milking and corn hoeing, without one moment of the precious twenty-four hours devoted to learning anything about his trade. The entries were all on one side of the ledger.

Such was the slavelike attitude of an apprentice that he rarely dared to complain, and John kept his peace until the time came for what he thought should be a final settlement. At the end of the second year he approached his master with a detailed statement showing that he had already worked all the time he was supposed to work at chores and cleaning up after Deborah. The only time he was not doing work of this kind was when he was working on his father's farm.

According to John's calculations, he was now privileged to devote his entire time until he became of age to learning how to make and repair clocks. He pleaded with Benjamin to carry out his part of the agreement and teach him something about the work—at least to allow him to look at the inside of a clock—something he had never seen. In reply Benjamin ordered him out to hoe the vegetables. John refused. This was a very daring act because Benjamin could have flogged the boy and the law would have been on his side. As John was still a minor he had no legal rights as an individual. If his father had attempted to sue Cheney and compel him to carry out his part of the contract, the master had a fool-proof and time-tried defense. All he had to do was to say that the apprentice was too stupid or too lazy to learn. That defense would fall on receptive ears. Slaves, indentured servants and apprentices constituted more than a token of wealth in a country where there was little currency and land was of uncertain value. The good solid citizen believed that the whole economy of the community would topple if the arbitrary rights of the master over the apprentice were amended in any way.

If Benjamin had had any physical courage he could have solved this problem by beating hell out of the apprentice and/or locking him up and putting him on a diet of bread and water. No matter what he did a little short of murder, the law and public opinion would have been on his side, just as later in the southern states law and public opinion were on the side of the plantation owner who mistreated his slaves. Very probably the paunchy, misshapen, sedentary clockmaker was afraid that if he tried to get tough the desperately goaded young apprentice might forget about the strict laws of Connecticut and give him a bloody nose. Confronted with this problem, Benjamin avoided the issue by the simple expedient of transferring his rights in the apprentice to his brother Timothy.

John had nothing to say about this arrangement but was very well pleased. Timothy Cheney was one of the most famous clocksmiths in Connecticut with a reputation for skill far above that enjoyed by his brother. John felt that he could learn more from Timothy than from Benjamin, and assumed that as he had already worked out more than his stint of chores the remainder of his period of service would be devoted to the learning of his trade. All that he had learned was a little about the making of brass buttons. Benjamin had been compelled to use his help when there was a rush order to be filled. In spite of two years of frustration and disappointment, his youthful hopes soared again and he agreed to extend his apprenticeship beyond the twenty-first year so that he could have the benefit of Timothy's teaching for a few additional months.

By moving from the home of one Cheney brother to the other, John escaped the foul drunkenness of Deborah but had to suffer the almost incredible penuriousness of Timothy. There hadn't been much to eat at Benjamin's home but there was less at his brother's. Timothy said grace before every meal and always managed to work in some pious remarks about the sins of gluttony.

He did not eat very much, ate very fast and as soon as he was finished would push back his plate and return thanks. That was a signal that the meal was over and no one dared eat another mouthful. As the poor apprentice was naturally the last to be allowed to help himself from the common bowl, he had to gobble his food in a hurry or endure the distress that only youth with an empty belly can suffer. Many years later, in his curious self-revealing autobiography, he said there was probably no one in the world who could eat faster than he could. The only times when he was able to satisfy his hunger were when Timothy was away on business and he and Mrs. Cheney could eat a decent meal. Those occasions were rare. When he was past middle age Fitch recalled one of the providential absences of the master. Mrs. Cheney feasted him with a dish of boiled potatoes and he ate almost as much as he wanted.

His position in Timothy's house was just as unsatisfactory as it had been in Benjamin's. According to the letter of the laboriously negotiated contract, he had more than fulfilled his obligations to do chores. He felt that Timothy was obligated now to teach him his trade. Timothy not only refused to do this but kept his tools locked up and would not allow the apprentice inside the shop. John learned nothing about clockmaking and actually ended his apprenticeship without ever seeing the inside of a clock.

All that he learned from the Cheney brothers out of three years of unpaid labor was a little about the making of brass buttons and buckles. His new master, Timothy, put him to work on his farm and when John rebelled piled more work on him and cut his food to the starvation point.

When he was sure that he had broken the spirit of his apprentice, the cruel and avaricious Timothy offered to release him for forty dollars and to give him a one-day holiday so that he could canvass his relatives and friends and borrow the money.

Chapter VI

BETTER TOOLS FOR THE FARMER

THE pioneer American hated Indians and trees with almost equal intensity. Both had to be cleared out before he could feel any sense of security in his new home. In a way the trees presented the greater difficulties. By stockades and forts, by friendly treaties and by bloody forays into their territories he could protect himself against the Indians, but before the soil could be completely cultivated the trees had to be destroyed. With unbroken forests stretching for hundreds of miles this at first appeared to be such a monumental task that the early settlers did not undertake it.

For many years they followed the Indian custom of setting fire to the dead grass in the autumn, thus burning off the underbrush and small trees and killing some of the larger ones. This left some bare unshaded spots where holes could be dug with wooden spades and corn planted in the spring. It was a long time before there were cleared patches large enough to institute planting in rows. A herring or a shad planted with the corn provided the fertilizer, if any was needed. The Pilgrims followed this practice for ten years before they had a patch of land large enough to justify the purchase of a single plow which was imported from England.

Some fields were cleared without chopping down a single tree. The farmer planted between the dead trees, which eventually rotted to the ground and the roots decayed so that after twenty or thirty years the land was ready for the plow. This delay was not so important as it would appear

to be, for the primitive wooden plow drawn by oxen was
not very much more effective than the wooden spade. It did
little more than scratch a rough shallow furrow in the loose
soil and hoes and spades had to be used to complete the
preparation of the soil for planting. There must have been
many sore backs and blistered hands around Plymouth Rock,
for the Pilgrims were largely composed of small business
men who had gone broke during the economic depression
in England. They were poor farmers and their descendants
continued to be poor farmers down to the present day. On the
other hand, the Indians were good agriculturists for they
had through the generations preserved and improved their
principal crop—corn—which must be planted each spring,
since it does not reseed itself. The Indians also grew pump-
kins, squash, beans, tobacco and other crops. As digging
tools they used the horns of deer and elk and the shoulder
blade of the buffaloes, tools not inferior to the crude wooden
tools of the colonists.

In many places the annual burning of the underbrush
became a kind of festive event. By building encircling fires
game both large and small was driven towards a central
point where they were easily killed, thus providing a kind of
secondary harvest. This was exactly the same kind of an
autumn game hunt the Chinese enjoyed for centuries before
the birth of Christ when the region around the Yellow River
was covered with forests as dense as those found in America.
In one of these autumn bonfires near Salisbury, Connecticut,
an Indian was caught in the encircling flames, could not
escape and was incinerated. The incident is noted in the
Salisbury chronicles but with no extravagant expression of
regret. Doubtless there were many other such holocausts

which were not considered of sufficient importance to warrant the sharpening of a quill pen.

The Pilgrims were followed by other immigrants who did not have to learn farming from the Indians—men who had farmed in England, or at least were saturated with farm traditions. As wider spaces were cleared of trees, they made more plows and wooden-toothed harrows and bred more oxen to draw them. For almost two hundred years they were content with these clumsy and inefficient tools, but the first patent granted in the new world was for an agricultural tool, a scythe. This was invented about 1646 by Joseph Jenks, a famous ironworker of colonial days and he was granted a patent which gave him a monopoly of the manufacture of the scythe for a period of fourteen years. The scythe consisted of a long narrow blade similar to the scythes now in use. It represented a great improvement over the sickle shaped like a quarter moon, and Jenks built up a prosperous manufacturing business at Pawtucket, Rhode Island. These New England scythes were so superior that many of them were shipped to Pennsylvania and bar iron returned in payment. It was not until about a hundred and fifty years later that some one thought of attaching a series of wooden fingers to the scythe and so making a cradle which would be useful in the reaping of wheat as well as the mowing of hay.

The replacement of the sickle by the scythe doubled the speed with which hay could be cut, but it required more manual labor, and, made with poor steel, the scythe was soon dulled. It became the custom to store the best barrel of hard cider on every farm, to be broached at harvest time when it was known as "the scythe sharpener." The haying season meant hard work but with a barrel of hard cider it became a festive event.

The clearing of the forests and the growing of crops went hand in hand, but axes came before plows. The first riches taken from the land were products of the forest, charcoal, tanbark and pearl ashes or potash. An acre of standing timber had to be felled and burned to produce a ton of potash, which sold for about twenty-five dollars. It was in this way that many a man provided himself with cash to buy lumber for his new home while clearing the ground for cultivation. The first Federal Patent Act was passed in 1790 "to promote the progress of science and useful arts." The first man to secure a patent was Samuel Hopkins of Vermont, who had devised a new method of making potash.

Improvement of tools for the forest were made more rapidly than improvement of tools for the farms. With thousands of square miles of forests to be cleared, it is not surprising that the first ax factory in the world should have been established on American soil. This was about 1820. Before that time all axes had been made to order by local blacksmith shops. Each blacksmith had his own method of tempering steel, and the best that could be said for these axes was that some were better than others. The customer fashioned his own handle from hickory he had cut and cured, and he also sharpened the blade. When it left the smithy the ax had no more of a cutting edge than could be made by hammers. The grinding alone meant at least one day's work by two men at a grindstone. Few axes were satisfactory. If not tempered enough they dulled easily and required constant sharpening. If too highly tempered they would crack and break.

Samuel W. Collins was a Connecticut hardware dealer who noted the universal demand for axes and the generally poor quality of those supplied and decided to go into the business of manufacturing them. After running a small shop in Hartford, Connecticut, for a few years, he later built a factory on the Farmington River which for more than a hundred years has been the world's largest producer of axes. His first methods did not differ much from those employed by the village smith, except that he used water power for trip hammers and for driving grindstones so that the purchaser got an ax that was already sharpened. A workman could turn out about eight axes a day. Each one was tempered separately.

Then Collins devised a method of tempering the axes in lots of one hundred, each receiving identical treatment. Two or three of the completed axes were tested and if they proved too brittle or too soft the whole lot was turned back into the furnace. For the first time in history a man could buy an ax of known quality and need have no fear that it would fail him when he was at work in the forest. That was the most important but only one of the many improvements. The tools turned out by the village shops had followed the lines of axes brought over from England—all were the same general weight and style. Collins began experimenting and devised an ax better suited to cutting into the hard woods of New England. As his range of customers widened, he made other axes to fill highly specialized demands, such as a light ax for the use of the southern turpentine workers. Soon he was doing an export business, making axes, adzes, machetes, cleavers, picks and other tools for Latin America. This was only one of many instances in which we secured the leadership in the manufacture of small articles of every-day use, while the great manufacturers of England and Europe devoted their attention to larger enterprises. We were shipping axes and hatchets all over the world long before the Civil War.

Curiously enough, although the farmer welcomed an improved ax and a better scythe, for generations his prejudices, ignorance and superstitions foiled all efforts to provide him with improved tools for working the soil. The plow he was using in 1800 was no better than the one used by the children of Israel, and the same could be said of all the other farm tools—harrows, rakes, spades and hoes. The reproduction capacity of the earth was a mystery to him—an annual miracle. He knew the routine part he had to play in the cycle of the seasons but only dimly understood the reasons. When the Indians taught the Pilgrims to plant a herring with a hill of corn they may have thought that this was some pagan rite, but it worked and they continued to follow it, without knowing the reason why, for they had no idea of the functions of a fertilizer. As manure piled up around a barn it was looked on as a nuisance and was disposed of in the easiest possible way, but was never spread on the fields. A later generation said that farmers would build a new barn rather than remove an old manure pile. The men who had seen a hill of corn thrive when planted with a herring did not know that well decayed horse dung would accomplish the same result. Without understanding the reason, they knew that some soil was barren and some soil was productive, and they assumed that the barren soil was poisoned. For some reason the superstition arose that iron would poison the soil and so as little as possible of it was used in strips on the wooden plow shares.

Twenty years after the Declaration of Independence plows were made as follows: "A winding tree was cut down, and a moldboard hewed from it; onto this was nailed the blade of an old hoe, or thin scraps of iron, or worn out horse shoes. The beam was usually a straight stick, the handles—split from the crooked trunk of a tree or as often cut from its branches. The beam was set at any pitch fancy might dictate."

At the time this clumsy instrument or something similar to it was in use on all the farms in America, Jefferson, whose interest in agriculture was more than political, invented an iron plow with a scientifically designed share. The French Institute gave him a decoration for this contribution to agriculture and French farmers plowed with plows of his design, but his fellow countrymen would have nothing to do with the contraption.

This indifference on the part of his fellow farmers did not lessen Jefferson's enthusiasm for an improved plow—for the use of iron instead of wood, for a moldboard scientifically designed and set at the right angle to send the plow at least three or four inches into the soil. While he was Secretary of State and President he encouraged Charles Newbold and others to work on improved plows but without any noticeable success. The farmers said and believed that iron plows would poison the soil, just as they later said and believed that hens would not lay on farms traversed by a railroad track. They did not completely disdain the use of iron; they nailed old hinges and other metal scrap on the wooden shares, but that was as far as they would go. This was more than a century and a half after the Pilgrims had learned their first lessons in agriculture from the friendly and hospitable Indians of the Massachusetts Bay Colony. There had been no progress during this period. The Indians had dug the ground with sharpened sticks or the horns of a deer. The Americans merely used a larger stick, shod with iron and dragged awkwardly through the ground by a team of oxen. Their favorite harrow was a thorn tree of convenient shape.

Jethro Wood was only one of many unhonored American inventors who designed better plows which no one would buy. The imaginations of Wood and other inventors of the early part of last century were stirred by the millions of unplowed acres which we were rapidly occupying, but the farmers were unresponsive. Wood's proposed plow followed Jefferson's idea but improved on it by providing a share made of two parts so that when the point was worn out it could be replaced. This greatly lengthened the life of the plow and made it actually cheaper than the homemade wooden contrivances. It also was more easily handled, would plow more soil in a day and plow it deeper. But the farmers would have none of it. His patent was taken out in 1819 and twenty-five years later he died in poverty.

Even Daniel Webster adhered to the conventional idea and his famous plow embodied all of the old and none of the new ideas, just being a larger machine than the others. It was in 1836 that he invented or designed a plow and had the implement constructed under his own supervision. It was, in comparison with the other plows of the period, like a monster of a modern military tank compared to a two-door sedan. It was twelve feet long, four feet wide and required the traction of four teams of oxen. Six or seven of Daniel's neighbors had to help him hold the plow in its furrow. Having demonstrated that his plow would turn the stubborn soil of his Marshfield, Massachusetts, farm, Daniel turned to his fellow plowmen and characteristically made a speech.

"When I have hold of the handles of my big plow in such a field," he said, "with four pair of cattle and hear the roots creak and see the stumps all go off under the furrow out of sight, and observe the clean mellowed surface of the plowed land, I feel more enthusiasm over my achievement than comes from my encounters in public life in Washington."

The machine plowed a furrow as mighty as the wave of the great Daniel's eloquence—two feet wide and twelve to fourteen inches deep. The plow was made entirely of wood, the share being covered with thin strips of iron.

In the same year that Webster guided his giant plow through his swampy land, plow history was being made in Illinois. John Deere, a strong young blacksmith, had moved there from Vermont and in his new home became acquainted with a type of soil unknown in New England. It was a rich black loam sheathed by a primeval sod so tough that no wooden plow could cut it. The sticky loam caked on ordinary plows and made them unworkable. The settlers from New England who had pushed out to the West were baffled by this strange manifestation of nature. A great many of the early visitors to the prairie country referred to it as a "land ocean" and assumed that the land would never be cultivated. Farmers cleared the isolated patches of timber land for farms and left the great stretches of prairies uncultivated. The thick sod which covered the rich soil could not be broken with an iron pointed wooden plow. One man wrote:

"The prairies, although generally fertile, are so very extensive that they must for a great length of time, and perhaps forever, remain wild and uncultivated."

Deere, who was a giant of a man, was not intimidated by the physical difficulties of the prairie soil. Jefferson and Jethro Wood and others had worked on iron plows which were adequate for the loose soils of the Atlantic seaboard, but the tough prairie sod demanded steel and John Deere made plows of it. He bought old sawmill blades with which he made self scouring plows which cut through the soil as clean as a razor. The heavy matted sod was cut by a steel disk attached to the beam. Unlike a great many other inventors, he was a good salesman and business man, and soon built up a good demand for his product. His plows were not light but in demonstrating them it was his custom to carry the plow to the field over his shoulders. Not many of his customers could do this and doubtless this sensational feat of strength helped to break down the ancient prejudices. Deere had no difficulty selling his plows to the prairie farmers. The supply of worn-out sawmill blades was exhausted in a few years and he had to import rolled steel from England to supply his needs, because our mills could not produce steel of the right quality.

Deere's plow laid forever the myth that iron plows would poison the soil and led to the steady improvement in plows which Jefferson had dreamed of and worked for. Old wooden plows were discarded so rapidly that few are to be found in museums. New plows were invented to meet the needs of special soils, the cultivation of special crops and even special social conditions. The sulkey plow was an example of the latter, for it provided a seat on which the young son, the wife or the daughter of the farmer could ride while guiding the horses through the cornfield.

Chapter VII

PAUL REVERE—PIONEER INDUSTRIALIST

OF THE three men who on an April night of 1775 tried to warn the Sons of Liberty in Concord that the British troops were marching from Boston, two had the decidedly unpoetic and unmusical names of Dawes and Prescott. For that reason the American poet who produced so many quotable lines turned to the third member of the party, whose name rippled like a New England brook, and immortalized him for a deed he never accomplished. Every school child is familiar with the poem beginning:

> "Listen my children and you shall hear
> Of the midnight ride of Paul Revere."

As a matter of cold fact, as is disclosed in Esther Forbes' delightful book, Revere did not complete his ride to Concord to warn Sam Adams and John Hancock of their peril and was less deserving of fame than either of his two companions, Dawes or Prescott. On the way to Concord the British soldiers overtook him and stole his horse and he walked the rest of the way, arriving in time to hear the sound of musket shots while he was helping to carry some of the Sons of Liberty documents to a safe hiding place.

It is because of this dramatic presentation of one of the least important events of Revere's busy life that his real position as a pioneer American industrialist has been obscured. He was not a cowboy nor, as he has frequently been portrayed, a kind of a progenitor of the pony express rider, who about a hundred years later carried messages from St. Joseph to San Francisco in the record time of ten days. But he was a successful retail merchant and manufacturer who built the first smokestack in Boston and founded the first of America's heavy industries, establishing a business that has been in successful operation for more than a hundred and forty years.

During colonial days Paul Revere was a very capable young silversmith who prospered at his trade. The teapots, cups, spoons and other articles he made and marked with his sign are now treasured by museums and private collectors not only because of his fame but because they represent the very best of the silversmith's art of that time. A silver water pitcher which he made has that combination of utility and beauty which makes a good piece of merchandise and for more than a century has probably outsold every pattern of water pitcher made in America. Millions of copies of it have been made in glass and porcelain and it is still a standard item in most department stores. He was also a successful manufacturer of household hardware; a bell caster, one of the first American manufacturers of ship gear, the first to roll copper, and the first to compete successfully with well-established and experienced metal workers of England.

The silversmith of colonial days was a much more important person than the name would indicate for he performed some of the functions of a mint. Coins were scarce and paper currency in well deserved disrepute. On the other hand, an ounce of good solid silver had a certain well established value whether it was coined into a Spanish dollar bearing the head of a Spanish king or fashioned into a spoon or became a part of a pair of candlesticks. Silver spoons, teapots and other objects of that sort represented savings of standard value which could always be turned into cash or bartered for other things on favorable terms. The customers of the silversmith were those who had savings in the form of silver articles which they brought to him for repair or to be made into something else. There were very limited opportunities to buy new things and it appears that a great many of the well-to-do satisfied their desire for novelty or change by having a silver teapot made into a pair of candlesticks or a set of silver spoons made into a tray or a tray into a teapot. The result was that the local silversmith knew more about the financial standing of his townspeople than anyone else. He also knew the trend in popular taste for luxury merchandise. When there was a stable currency and mints were established and banks organized, the silversmith suffered something in prestige. His art remained the same but his customers changed. They were no longer the thrifty who wanted their silver savings hammered into some useful form, but the spendthrift wealthy looking for objects of frivolous value.

Perhaps Revere foresaw that this change would come if the hopes of the Sons of Liberty were realized and a prosperous new America developed with the coming of independence for which they were plotting. He had several sons growing up whom he wanted to establish in a business more secure than the one he had followed, and so in 1783 he set up a small retail shop in Boston. It was stocked with a variety of English goods ranging from wall paper to hardware. The order included some Sheffield plate, a new product which was offering ruinous competition to the proud London silversmiths. He did not, like some other Boston merchants, trade with the enemy by the purchase of goods from England while we were still at war with her. But he did send his orders through a friend in London with instructions that the goods were to be shipped as soon as the treaty of peace was signed.

The goods Paul Revere ordered for his shop did not differ materially from the merchandise with which colonial shops had been stocked for a hundred years. Monopolies had stifled competition. Manufacturers saw no need to invent new merchandise or to change the design of old items. There were periodical changes in such luxury items as jewelry, silverware and clothing of the nobility, but the consumer goods of the ordinary man did not differ from one generation to the other. Radical changes in the stocks of retail shops did not come, as at present, as the result of a new invention or improved design but because of new merchandise discovered in odd corners of the world by venturesome sea traders. Merchandise from every corner of the globe can now be found in any American department store. But in Paul Revere's time a common blue and white ginger jar from China was the talk of the town either in Boston or London. Every ship returning from a strange port brought novelties in the form of merchandise that excited the imagination of artists as well as merchants. Some of the most inspiring merchandise came from China, changing the styles of furniture, porcelain and silverware. Stationers also found a new article to make and sell as the result of the visits of merchant vessels to Canton. There Englishmen and Americans saw envelopes for the first time. The Chinese had for centuries been insuring the secrecy of letters and documents by placing them in sealed envelopes, but no one else had thought of this simple device.

Revere was one of the first American retail merchants to see the advantages of specialization and as stock sold out and new orders were placed he did not reorder some of the lines.

Soon the hardware items were crowding out the others doubt-less because he felt he was able to judge their quality and workmanship, since they were made of metal, but he was no expert on textiles or paper. In fact, his first advertisement announcing the opening of the shop featured "hardware goods consisting of pewter, brass and copper." He soon came to the conclusion that he could manufacture many of those small imported items at a cost much less than the price he had to pay the English manufacturers; and at an age when most prosperous men think about retiring, he made plans for a career as a manufacturer. As he considered the possibilities of this new business, he began to lose interest in the silver shop which had supported his family for many years.

The first smokestack to send soot over Boston came from Revere's "Furnass" which he set up in the shipbuilding dis-trict. Even during the time that the foundry was under construction his plans had expanded. In addition to making the easily fabricated lines of household hardware, he made preparations to produce anvils, hammers, hearths, spikes and all of the other gear demanded by Boston's rapidly expanding shipbuilding industry. In fact he made out of iron a great amount of ship gear such as cogs, spikes, and braces, etc., which should have been made of brass and copper. As no one in America knew how to work these two metals, all gear of this sort had to be imported. In this boom period of American shipbuilding, the American shipwrights were using poorly seasoned timbers, iron hardware instead of brass. They didn't have time to wait for the proper materials. English ship-wrights poked fun at these ships but they sailed and the ship-building business was profitable. Revere was so entranced by this new work that he moved his family into a house next to the mill.

The silversmith turned ironmaster appeared to have enjoyed a return of youth and energy and ambitions. Almost as soon as he had mastered the comparatively simple process of iron casting, he went in for brass casting so that American ships could be as well equipped as any on the seas, as they soon were. In the first work of this sort he undertook, the recasting of the cracked bell in his own church, he merely broke up, melted and cast the metal from the old bell, supplemented by other scrap which he could buy and some silver which well-to-do members of the church donated. The recasting of cracked bells was a steady part of his business, for while good bells were made in England, there were few good bell ringers in America and clumsy sextons broke many bells. With scrap metal from other sources he cast ship bells and he made from copper or brass the spikes and other ship gear he had formerly made of iron.

As his business grew, he could no longer depend on the supply of scrap that came from cracked bells and old sailing ships that had been broken up. He had to work out his own formula for alloys to produce the different kinds of brass, copper, and bronze combinations he needed for the various kinds of articles he was manufacturing. All this information could be learned today from the textbooks in any high school library. But at this time these were secrets known only to the great manufacturers in England and Europe. Progress was stifled by a fear of competition which made everyone aggressively secretive about valuable special skills of this kind. It was an age of jealousy, envy, and suspicion during which even scientists concealed their discoveries.

It is curious that no one in New England knew how to work copper. A deposit of copper had been discovered in Granby, Connecticut, in 1705 and workmen were brought from the kingdom of Hanover to work the mine and operate a smelter. Since the English law prohibited the smelting of copper in the colonies, this was a daring bootleg enterprise which was carried on with varying degrees of success for a number of years. In 1737 James Higley made copper coins which cleverly evaded the law against counterfeiting. One side of the coin was stamped: "I am good copper," the other "Value me as you will." The enterprise later fell on evil days. A clergyman was employed as manager. He was not very successful for it was said of him that he "seemed to have known more about the fires of hell than of smelting furnaces." At the time Paul Revere wrestled with the problem of copper alloys, the ore at Granby had been worked out and the abandoned mine was used as a prison for captured Tories. What had been learned by preceding generations about the working of copper had been forgotten.

There was no master metallurgist to whom the veteran silversmith could apprentice himself in the hope that he would be taught which of the "seven metals," and in what proportions, should be mixed with copper so that it would be malleable and could be drawn into the bolts and spikes and other findings so necessary for the building of American ships. In default of this he set out to discover the secret by the trial and error method, and in a very short time he had succeeded.

One more thing was needed to make American shipbuilding completely self contained, and that was copper sheathing —so necessary for the protection of the bottoms of wooden boats and procurable only in England. One daring American had tried the experiment of sending an unsheathed ship to sea. The experiment was a failure. Before many days had passed the hull was so encrusted with barnacles that even in a stiff breeze it could make only two miles an hour. It would undoubtedly have foundered in a storm. If it had not been able to reach port soon it would have become immobile like a ghost ship in the Sargossa Sea.

Having solved so many other problems successfully, Revere with considerable confidence planned to construct a copper rolling mill even before he was familiar with all the processes involved. No one in America knew anything about rolling copper at that time and there was no way of learning. The process was a secret held by great manufacturers in England and as long as they held this secret they controlled the production of copper sheathing and so held potential control of the world's shipbuilding. Americans had fortunes invested in shipping and were making other fortunes by building ships. But Great Britain, which was none too friendly, could cripple our entire shipping interests by the simple expedient of cutting off our supply of the one material with which ships could be bottomed.

At the age of sixty-five Revere started on his new venture— the building of a copper rolling mill which he was not quite sure he knew how to operate. He put all his money into it and the government loaned him ten thousand dollars and nineteen thousand pounds of copper to experiment with. As the many new problems arose, he solved them successfully. Within a year he was able to write to the Secretary of the Navy that he had succeeded and that his mill was in practical operation. He was a good salesman as well as a master crafts-man, and he started off with two good contracts. He rolled the copper for the dome of the State House in Boston and for the dome of the New York City Hall.

A pioneer in many things, Revere was also a pioneer in the payment of high wages. The men in his copper mill were paid two dollars per day, a sensationally high wage when one remembers that farm hands of that period got two dollars per week. Considering the average wages paid at that period his scale of two dollars a day was much more daring and liberal that the five dollar wage announced by Henry Ford more than a hundred years later. Revere's explanation of this high wage was that he "wanted his men to be contented." Having been a workman himself he had a lively sympathy for workmen. There were few labor troubles in America when the industries were run by former workmen who were in daily personal contact with their men. Disputes began when financiers gained control of industries others had founded.

About the time his rolling mill began successful operations, the *Constitution*, the most powerful battleship flying the American flag, was brought into Boston for a complete overhauling in preparation for the campaign against the Algerian pirates who had humiliated us by making us pay tribute for the privilege of sailing our ships in waters of the Mediterranean. Thanks to the development of Revere's copper mills, the American navy was now completely independent of foreign supplies. He manufactured all the bolts and pumps and other gear as well as the copper sheathing. The whole country had been stirred by Pinckney's defiant "not a damned cent for tribute," and it followed the refitting of the great battleship with intense interest. The men worked overtime on the job of getting the ship into fighting trim in record time. The log of the *Constitution* for June 26, 1803, contains the following entry:

"The carpenters gave nine cheers, which was answered by the seamen and calkers because they had in fourteen days completed coppering the ship with copper made in the United States."

The commander was in such a hurry to get at the job of humbling the pirates that he sailed without approving Revere's bill for twenty-five thousand dollars. America's first heavy industry was well established and light industries were making slow but steady progress. Eli Whitney had successfully tried out his experiment with mass production. Revere was constructing copper boilers for Robert Fulton's steam engine. Eli Terry was making his plans to supply the nation with cheap clocks. A number of small mills were carding and spinning wool and cotton to be turned into cloth by hand operated looms. The power loom had been invented but had not been perfected. At hundreds of small forges pioneer ironmasters were learning how to treat the numerous varieties of iron found in the country. Encouraged by Revere's success with the copper rolling mills, someone projected an iron rolling mill, which was put into operation a few years later. Pottery was being produced in Vermont. Hundreds of mechanics were trying to invent machines which would lessen hand labor and enable us to make the things we had heretofore had to import. We had been enjoying political independence for twenty years but were just beginning to develop economic independence—just beginning to free ourselves from foreign manufacturers by developing our own factories.

Few of the colonists who were so righteously indignant about the iniquitous British restrictions realized that manufacturing required a great deal of technical skill. Old Sam Adams appeared to think that as soon as restrictions were removed prosperous and busy factories would spring into being just as the mayflower bloomed in New England woods soon after the snows melted. Of all the Boston patriots who had worked and plotted for independence, Revere was the only one who had the skill and experience to be a manufacturer. Others had talked louder and longer about the new America they were planning to build, but Revere made the largest contribution to it.

Chapter VIII

NAILS AND TACKS AND SCREWS

IN THE historic year of 1776 Jeremiah Wilkinson of Rhode Island was the talk of the neighborhood in which he lived because of what was known at the time as his "invention." The fact that his simple adaptation of an old method of doing things should have been looked on as an invention, and that his name should have become fixed in the folklore of American industry shows very graphically the great advance we have made since that time in manufacturing processes. Wilkinson was a tackmaker and like other tackmakers in all parts of the world he cut thin strips from sheet iron, with a pair of shears, snipped the strips into lengths suitable for tacks and then headed each one by hand. A good worker could turn out two thousand tacks in a day. They were not very good tacks and no one today would bother to use them, but they were then the best that could be had either here or in any other part of the world. Wilkinson's great invention consisted of nothing more than the device of securing a dozen or more embryo tacks into a vise at one time so that all could be headed with the same hammer blows. He later made nails in the same way. May his memory ever be green. At this late day this appears to be what anyone would have done. But generations had been making tacks and no one had ever thought of this simple labor-saving method.

It was a long time before any further progress was made in the manufacture of nails and tacks, but Jeremiah Wilkinson had shown that things could be done in a new way and had set fellow tackmakers and nailmakers to thinking along new and revolutionary lines. But for a generation or more nails and tacks were made in the same old way. In fact, while people were talking about the wonders of Robert Fulton's steamboat, which traveled between New York and Albany without sails, all of these articles were still being made by hand, laboriously and expensively. With a rapidly increasing population there was a demand for houses which has never been satisfied. Houses could not be built without nails, a large quantity of nails. All that could be made found a ready sale though at prices which were but a fraction less than they now bring at antique shops. At one time Thomas Jefferson, who was a tireless builder, kept a dozen nailmakers busy on his Monticello estate.

So great was the demand for nails that a curious piece of American folklore has been handed down about them. The story is that when old and decrepit housese were abandoned, it was customary to burn down the house in order to retrieve the nails. The story inevitably recalls that of Charles Lamb about the Chinese who burned down their houses in order to enjoy the suberb delicacy—roast pig. According to Lamb this led to the destruction of so many houses that the Emperor of China was compelled to prohibit the eating of roast pig. The two stories are probably equally fanciful, but there is no doubt but that when a house *did* burn, the ashes were carefully raked over to retrieve the nails which could be used in rebuilding. They were too valuable to be allowed to rust into nothingness. The forging of the nails required for building a house probably demanded as many man hours of labor as the erection of the house itself.

Even this handmade production of tacks and nails was

during the colonial days severely frowned upon by the British authorities. In 1750 a report to Parliament disclosed the fact that there were two iron slitting mills in Massachusetts producing rods from which nails and spikes were made. Parliament reacted in the usual way by outlawing these mills and at the same time took occasion to encourage the export of American pig iron to England, where it would feed the mills to make articles for sale to the colonists. The theory of colonial economy was that we should produce pig iron which we would ship, to England to be returned to us later in the form of nails and tacks and other products of British manufacture. Lord North, Chancellor of England, boasted that if he could have had his way about it he would have made it impossible for the colonists to hammer out a single nail. He considered it his duty to protect the interests of a very large group of British workmen. Nailmaking provided a livelihood for sixty thousand Britons, all of whom hammered them out by hand, just as we did, and just as the Romans had done when Britain was a Roman colony. They sold the nails to us for more than twenty cents a pound. Actually nails were so valuable that prices were not quoted by the pound but by the dozen or the hundred.

It appears to have been a long time before anyone ever thought of producing nails except by adaptations of the old hand methods. Indeed automatic metal-working machinery of any kind was impossible to visualize because no one had ever seen an automatic machine other than a cotton gin or a spinning jenny. It was possible to think of a pliable material like thread or yarn being worked by machinery but metals had never been shaped except by blows of the smith's hammer. Few people thought this method would ever be changed. The American statesmen of the early days of the country were all sanguine about our being able to do without imported articles but they hoped and thought that this would be accomplished by means of home industries, hand labor at living wages which would be accompanied by steady employment. The British nailmakers about whose welfare Lord North was so solicitous were by no means prosperous, and his concern may also have been over the burden of taxes borne by the wealthy. All British workmen were paid wages so close to the subsistence level that the workingman class made heavy drains on what were known as the "poor funds." Many British economists believed that low wages were necessary to maintain the country's growing export trade, that between a living wage and poor relief the latter represented the lesser evil. If nailmakers were thrown out of employment it would mean a heavier drain on these public funds.

The American way of life as envisaged by our statemen differed from this pattern only in that they believed in a living wage instead of doles to the poor. The British capitalists who were growing rich on shipping and the export trade feared that higher wages would make it impossible to compete in foreign trade. Whether or not it was designed for that purpose, relief to the poor constituted a kind of a subsidy to labor. We wanted to develop manufactures of our own but thought of them only as following the British methods of hand labor. Freedom from this sweatshop form of labor did not come from signers of the Declaration of Independence or any of the statesmen of the first few decades of independence. It was brought about by a large number of inventors and petty manufacturers, some of whom built up big factories. Their purpose was to make merchandise which by its cheap price could be sold in large quantities and so provide adequate profits. In no utterance by a public man in the seventeenth century do we find a hint that anyone had any conception of the part machinery was to play in the production of useful merchandise which would stock the shelves of the retail dealers and supply the needs of millions of consumers.

In 1789 when it was proposed to put a duty on imported spikes, nails, tacks, and brads, Fisher Ames, of Massachusetts, said in Congress:

"This manufacture, with very little encouragement, has grown up remarkably. It has become common for the country people in Massachusetts to erect small forges in their chimney corners, and in the winter and in the evenings when little other work can be done, great quantities of nails are made, even by children. These people take the rod of iron of the merchant and return him the nails; and, in consequence of this easy mode of barter the manufacture is prodigiously great. These advantages are not exclusively in the hands of the people of Massachusetts. The business might be prosecuted in a similar manner in every state exerting equal industry."

The production of nails came to the attention of Alexander Hamilton who said, in 1791, that the United States already produced a very large part of the nails and spikes needed for home use and could produce all. He was thinking, of course, of the industrious farmers who worked by their forges at the kitchen hearth. The spinning jenny had been in successful operation for some time and the power loom was being perfected. Whitney's cotton gin was still being talked about. The British imagination did not go any farther than the power loom and other textile machinery. It remained for us to develop practically all the improved machines for working both wood and metal.

These early inventors and small manufacturers were known and honored in their own community and generation, but with a very few exceptions the records of their ambitions, activities, and accomplishments are incomplete, inaccurate or ignored. Throughout the greater part of last century the only people considered important enough to form biographical material were dull and dreary statesmen and even more dull and dreary divines. The successful businessmen and industrialists were ignored. It was not until more than a hundred years after the death of Paul Revere that an adequate biography of this great man was written. In the meantime hundreds of biographies of lesser Bostonians had been published.

In the absence of written records of men who were too obscure to attract the attention of historians and too busy or too illiterate to write diaries, there has grown up a great but unexplored folklore about early American inventors and manufacturers. Men drew plans of machines which could not be made because of lack of tools, ignorance of metallurgical processes, or lack of technical skill. These plans were like those for the airplane which was dreamed of and designed centuries before it was possible to build one. As early as 1809 Ezra l'Hommedieu of Saybrook wrote the Secretary of the Treasury that he had invented a machine that would make 300 pounds of screws a day with the labor of one man and a boy. A great many inventors of those days thought up intricate machines for which they could not draw the designs and many of the designs which were drawn could not be translated into workable machines. Ezra's invention must have fallen into one of those categories for he never made any screws by machine.

At a later date Abraham Lincoln patented what appears

to have been a completely impractical device for dragging flatboats over shoals. In any event, his machine was never put into practical operation. That was true of a very large proportion of the thousands of inventions for which patents were secured. Many were impractical to start with. Others could be made workable only after great sums had been spent on research and experiment. In the early days of our developing industries there were no manufacturers with capital enough to carry out these experiments nor was there the technological skill necessary to convert an idea into a machine. The result was that many of the early inventors, whose ideas may have been born sound and practical, never saw their machines in operation.

There are stories that Jacob Perkins of Newburyport, Massachusetts, in 1795 made a machine that would turn out ten thousand nails a day. About that time a Pittsburgh, Pennsylvania, manufacturer advertised machine-made nails "as good as those made by hand." But during the next thirty years neither Pittsburgh nor Newburyport produced any appreciable quantity of nails. Probably more credence can be given to the story that Ezekiel Reed of Bridgewater, Massachusetts, invented a machine which about 1825 was making tacks at the rate of a hundred million a year. Some of these early inventors of nailmaking machines tried to make nails of cast iron, producing an iron object which looked like a nail but was very difficult to drive without breaking. This excited a prejudice against machine-made nails which persisted long after their manufacture had been perfected. Some of the early machines required such a large amount of hand labor that but little savings in cost were effected. The machine would shape a point and head the nail but the specially prepared bar had to be fed into it by hand. This was considered a great advance over old methods and a patent office report commented pridefully on the fact that nails were now being made with "no more labor than is necessary to supply the rod of iron to machine."

There were many machines invented, each inventor profiting by the mistakes of his predecessors and the constantly increasing skills of the workmen. Finally, about 1825 perfectly satisfactory nails and spikes were being produced by machinery and the household production of nails gradually disappeared. The machine-made nails were so cheap that they were sold by the pound instead of by the hundred, and soon the production was being measured in kegs and casks. A cheap and plentiful supply of nails was the first important contribution to cheap and comfortable housing—marking an advance in the standard of living which we were soon sharing with other countries. In 1842 we exported from New York 6,344 casks of nails and the following year 9,248 casks. A hundred years after Lord North had determined that we should make no nails, we were not only making all the nails we needed, but exporting increasing quantities of them. About the same time we began the equally successful export of nuts and bolts. That was the beginning of our export of small metal manufactured products. In the same year we began producing at Providence, Rhode Island, the first screws ever to be made by machinery.

The manufacture of cut nails had just been established on a sound basis when the invention of the wire nail brought a complete revolution in the industry. The first wire nail machines were as clumsy as the first machine for making cut nails, but as the machines were perfected they worked at such lightning speed that a single one would produce four hundred nails a minute. Other machines had to be invented to weigh automatically this torrent of nails, place them in kegs and haul the kegs away. The change from cut to wire nails was spectacular. In 1886 we produced six hundred thousand kegs of wire nails and more than eight million kegs of cut nails. Ten years later the production of wire nails was almost six million kegs, that of cut nails a little more than two million kegs.

The manufacture of horseshoe nails was a more difficult proposition. Nails used in building houses were just hammered into the wood and were left there until the house burned or was torn down. Nails which affixed shoes to the hoof of a horse were subject to the same strains and stresses as the gadgets which fix a motor car tire to the wheel. They had to be tough. It was not until about 1850, many years after successful house nails had been manufactured by machinery, that anyone invented a machine to make what were known as "horse nails." Silas S. Putnam of Neponset, Massachusetts, invented a machine and made nails. The saving in cost of manufacture was enormous. A skillful and hard-working blacksmith could produce ten to twelve pounds of horse nails a day. Mr. Putnam's machine would turn out a hundred to a hundred and fifty pounds of nails in the same time.

There wasn't anything particularly novel about his invention as he had only adapted the idea of using a trip hammer instead of a hammer manipulated by hand by a smith. The smith gave the handmade nails twenty hammer blows. Putnam's machine gave them sixty. But no one would buy Putnam's nails. There was no name for it then, but we know it now as "sales resistance." It wasn't until the Civil War that machine-made horse nails were adopted generally, just as were machine-made shoes. The Boston Light Artillery was sent to Baltimore and possibly because Putnam had the only large supply of horse nails in Boston, the cavalry steeds were shod with his nails, known as "Putnam Horse Nails." Much to the surprise of everyone, including Putnam's Bostonian neighbors, the nails stood up remarkably well. The matter came to the attention of the Quartermaster General and soon Putnam had to enlarge his factory to fill the contract for horse nails for a very large part of the Union Army.

Chapter IX

THE YANKEE PEDDLER

Even before they were producing more than a trickle of merchandise American manufacturers departed from old world methods in the disposal of the goods they made for sale. In communities of England and on the continent of Europe the population was static, except as depleted by migrations to the new world. The same families lived in the same places for generations and lived about the same kind of lives. The butchers, the bakers, and the candlestick makers had the same customers year after year, consisting of the sons and grandsons of the men their fathers and grandfathers had served. So did the tailor, the tinsmith, and the shoemaker. Each community was self-contained so far as craftsmen and customers were concerned. There was no business to be done outside, little hope of adding to the narrow circle of customers in the community. The craftsmen enjoyed the security which comes with the absence of competition, but they also suffered the stagnation and lack of enterprise that security entails. In some instances the craft guilds, which were more powerful and more abitrary than an American labor union, provided a monopoly for the local artisan by severely restricting the territory in which members of their guild could work.

The situation in America both as regards manufacturers and customers was quite different. Populations were constantly changing, trade channels were not frozen, there were no monopolistic guilds, and there was a general shortage of men with any mechanical skill. New communities were springing up every year and old communities were growing and changing. Many towns were comparatively prosperous but did not have enough local artisans to make the wares that were needed. And so from the very beginning of our national life we had an interchange of trade between different communities the like of which was unknown in other countries. The owner of a shop or the traveling craftsman was free to seek customers wherever he thought he could find them, and often they were to be found only after long and difficult journeys.

As a result of those conditions, American enterprise in selling and ingenuity in merchandising were developed before we were a nation. Connecticut craftsmen in early colonial days made articles of household utility not only for their neighbors but for sale in other and often distant places. The brothers Edward and William Pattison, who owned and operated a tinsmith shop in Connecticut are credited with being the first American manufacturers to look for markets away from home and so were the first of the historic line of Yankee peddlers. The practice of tinsmiths from the inception of the trade was to keep few if any wares in stock and to fabricate utensils for customers who called at the shop and placed their orders. There were, of course, many periods of idleness, as there were in all the small shops conducted in this fashion. The Pattison brothers were projected into trade expansion because of the fact that they were the only tinsmiths in a wide area. With what was obviously a consistent demand for tinware in a radius of a hundred miles or more from their shop, they did not wait for customers. When they had made up enough tinware to provide a load, one of the brothers would start out with a pack on his back, calling on all the homes in the neighborhood. As their business grew, the brothers devoted their attention to manufacturing and employed venturesome young men who, by 1776, were covering routes of 1500 miles and creating new customers for the only large scale industry in Connecticut.

Other tinsmiths who were attracted to the new country followed the same selling methods. The Yankee tinsmith, who established a tradition called himself a "whitesmith," and was a complete manufacturing and selling unit in himself. He dipped the sheets of iron into the molten tin, cut, bent, and soldered the pie dish or baking tin, and then went out himself or sent out his peddlers to sell the wares. His product had little resemblance to the tinware that can now be bought in any five and ten cent store, but it found a ready market at prices that today would be considered outrageously high. The tinsmith's profit on the individual item was small, but he did a large volume of business, prospered, and established a tradition for American manufacturing and merchandising methods.

As the Connecticut manufacturers began producing a wider variety of saleable merchandise, peddling became a specialized occupation. Some schoolteachers, like Louisa M. Alcott's father, strapped packs on their backs during the school vacation period and traveled through the country selling tinware and other small, easily transported articles. Mr. Alcott did not make a fortune, but many of the early peddlers later became successful and wealthy businessmen. Collis P. Huntington, who played such a prominent part in the building of the Southern Pacific Railway, began his business career as a peddler.

The original packs consisted entirely of tinware but they soon began to contain a variety of items, most of them made in Connecticut. Brass buttons, sewing thread, needles, "gal-luses," combs, pins, and thimbles gave variety to the travel-ing shop. The sources of supply were the small Connecticut factories which began making these notions and sold them successfully in competition with the more expensive im-ported articles. The peddler was usually able to offer his wares at a price less than the housewife had been accustomed to paying and in this way the new wares of the pioneer American factories received a wide distribution under very favorable circumstances.

For several generations in different parts of the country the Yankee peddler performed most of the functions of mer-chandising that are now performed by large and complex, but more efficient, organizations. The housewife hoarded her nickels and dimes and awaited the peddler's arrival to replenish her supply of sewing material and small house-hold articles. It was through him that people on the ever advancing frontier learned of the new products that were constantly being turned out by the New England factories. It was also through him that many people heard about what was happening in the outside world.

He was a welcome visitor at every farm home. His arrival was often the signal to stop all other activities while every-one crowded around to see his dazzling display of merchan-dise and listen to his stories. No commercial traveler ever had a more receptive customer or a smaller expense account. No matter where he happened to be at night the peddler was certain to be offered lodging, supper, and breakfast. If, before he left, he gave the housewife a handkerchief or a spool of sewing silk, he had observed all the amenities and settled his obligations in a way satisfactory to all concerned. In fact, the entertainment of the peddler in frontier communities was just as much of a social obligation as the entertainment of the itinerant preacher, but with a rather important exception. The preacher was sure of a welcome only in the homes of those of his own sect. The peddler was welcome everywhere.

In these days of encyclopedic mail order catalogs and five and ten cent stores just around the corner, it is difficult to realize what an important function the peddler performed. A hundred and fifty years ago the wageless trade of the housewife might have been seriously upset by the loss of a needle or the exhaustion of the supply of sewing threads. The nearest shop with a stock of needles and thread might be distant a day's journey.

At first the Connecticut peddlers did not get much farther than the New York state line. Pennsylvania peddlers at a later date traveled throughout the state and penetrated the frontier to sell stockings and caps. Benedict Arnold, who appears to have worked out new trade routes for himself, traveled north into Canada where he sold caps and cheese. He must have been a successful peddler for he amassed enough capital to go into the West India trade. As horse trails were opened up the peddler carried a larger stock in saddlebags and traveled farther from home. With the building of steamboats the peddlers developed new sales territory, some going as far as St. Louis and New Orleans. In a way they initiated the modern warehousing system, for stocks of goods would be shipped to points in the South and West to be stored until their arrival.

The peddler became a national institution, the butt of many a joke, the theme of many a song and story. A versifier of a century ago asked, "Why is the dust in such a rage?" and then supplied the answer:

"It is the yearly caravan
Of peddlers, on their pilgrimage
To Southern parts, full of Japan
And tin, and wooden furniture.
That try to charm the passing eye
And spices which, I am very sure
Ne'er saw the shores of Araby
Well skilled in that smooth eloquence
Are they, to steal away your pence."

By the time these verses appeared in print the peddler with a pack on his back had disappeared in all but the most backwoods parts of the country. The peddler of 1850 carried a larger stock and traveled with a horse and wagon. Instead of acting as agent for the manufacturers or taking goods on consignment, they bought their own stocks. Many of them prospered and established country stores. Jim Fisk, the Wall Street wizard of odorous memory, was one of the most successful. He started his business career as a street peddler but soon saved enough money to buy a team and wagon with which he toured the countryside. He was partner in a Boston retail store before establishing himself in New York. Some manufacturers used spectacular peddling methods to introduce a new line of goods. The proprietors of a pottery in Vermont loaded four-horse wagons with their wares and sent them out with silk-hatted salesmen.

The peddler carried his merchandise with him, demonstrated the quality of the goods, made the sale, and collected the money. That is, sometimes he collected money but often he took his pay in beeswax or some other farm produce. It was very simple and at the same time a very expensive method of merchandising. The difference between the cost of an article manufactured in New Haven or Waterbury,

Connecticut, and the price charged for it in Louisiana or Missouri was of necessity very great. The peddler, even if he had a horse and wagon, carried a very small cargo, his daily sales ran to only a few dollars and he had to take a big mark-up on his costs. But for several generations the belief persisted that peddled wares were cheap.

With inadequate merchandising methods and inefficient machinery for distribution, this was the only way that sales in a new field could be made. There was no conception of any such terms as "consumer acceptance." The idea that goods could be sold on the basis of an established reputation for quality was strange and new during this transition stage from workshop to factory production. A cabinetmaker might have a reputation for good workmanship that extended beyond his own village. But even that did not mean that the chair or table he made would be accepted without careful examination. When all merchandise was made by hand it could not be uniform in quality, and there were usually slight variations in design. The customer must see and examine before he would buy. It was not until manufacturers began the mass production of trade-marked goods which they sold by trade name backed by advertising that there was a supply of dependable merchandise of standard quality.

Eli Terry's merchandising methods provided the first example of this. He marked every one of his clocks with his own name and they soon acquired such a reputation for accuracy and reliability that people were willing to buy a Terry clock without actually seeing and examining the clock itself. This consumer confidence, backed by aggressive selling methods, enabled him to sell more clocks and thus reduce the unit price. The makers of brass buttons stamped their names on the buttons or made them with a distinctive design. And in this way the first savings in the cost of selling goods began to be effected. Often it meant nothing more than a saving in the time of the peddler. But as post offices and regular lines of transportation and retail stores were established, it meant that orders for goods could be placed by mail. The cost of selling has constantly gone down and with it the cost of goods to the consumer. Still, a great many Americans do not realize that the easier it is to sell an article, the more cheaply it can be sold.

With the growth of the country store the peddler began to outlive his usefulness and had to face a growing tide of organized opposition. Many of the states enacted laws requiring out-of-state peddlers to pay very high license fees for the privilege of doing business. These laws were designed not only to protect the interests of the country merchant but also to encourage the location of factories away from New England. The legislation was partially successful, for Jerome and some of the other early clockmakers shipped cases and parts of clocks to different parts of the South and West and had them assembled there.

The peddler has practically disappeared from American life and in remote parts of the country is encountered even more rarely than the horse and buggy. But he played an important part in the early trade of the country and his spirit of enterprise still lives in the American merchandising methods.

As the peddler disappeared from the scene, the agent who sold a single specialty took his place as a national character, but one held in less esteem.

The Civil War was a period when the agents flourished, not because of the war but because the methods of distribution had not caught up with the manufacture of the many new things that were being made and offered for sale. There had, as yet, been no national advertising worthy of the name. People did not accept new articles because of their faith in the name of the manufacturer—certainly not because an advertisement appeared in a reliable publication. The idea that a publisher should accept any responsibility for the claims which advertisers published in his columns had not yet developed. Even such staid publications as the *Youth's Companion* and *Harper's Weekly* allowed anyone to say his say— at space rates.

There was but one accepted method of introducing a new specialty and that was through agents who would call at homes and offices with the article for sale—make the sale, deliver the goods, and collect the money. It was expensive. It was the most expensive method of selling that has ever been used, but there was no other way until advertising began to play its part and retail shops stocked new merchandise in anticipation of sales. Newspapers of the period were full of advertisements for agents, promising big profits on the sale of articles of low unit cost. A typical one appeared in *Harper's Weekly* in January 1862:

"Agents for the Solar Matches wanted in places where not already appointed. Only those who can command a cash trade wanted. The right kind of a man treated with liberality. The Solar matches are now superseding all other matches now on the market as they contain no sulphur, have no unpleasant smell when burning and never miss fire and are as cheap as the suffocating sulphur matches. Already our factory is running day and night to fill orders. Solar Match Co., 101 Beekman Street, New York."

Assuming that the claims of the company to the superiority of their product were genuine, think what a different method of merchandising would be adopted today! Newspaper and magazine advertisements would tell of the new product. A demand could be created so that retail dealers would stock the new match which retailers could sell at a very small mark-up over the wholesale price. The small advertisement asking for agents probably cost only a few dollars. It would have cost thousands of dollars to put on a campaign appealing to the consumers, but in the end the Solar Match Company would have sold more matches, made more money, and the customer would have gotten his matches at a cheaper price.

An amazing variety of things were sold by agents. Kerosene, or "coal oil," as it was more generally known, was still something of a novelty. It had a reputation for being dangerously explosive. Any number of new wicks, burners, and chimneys were brought on the market for use in what were called "fluid lamps," all guaranteed to be non-explosive and all sold by agents.

With the start of the Civil War thousands of agents found a new article to sell which was nothing more than letter paper and envelopes, though it was soon dressed up in the form of prize packages which contained all kinds of worthless gadgets. With thousands of men in the military camps, their friends and relatives at home became letter writers. To most of them personal correspondence had always been confined to rare letters to distant relatives telling important family news, births and marriages and deaths. A dozen sheets of note paper and as many envelopes might last a family for years. But with fathers, sons, and husbands away, letters had to be written regularly. The family stock of stationery was soon exhausted.

Some enterprising Philadelphia job printer saw an opportunity. He put up packages of stationery and employed agents to go from house to house to sell them. He was highly successful, for there was little competition in this field. The stationery shops were mainly concerned with the manufacture and sale of blank books and other supplies for offices. There were no corner drugstores or news and cigar stands where one could purchase a box of writing paper. Selling package stationery through agents soon became a business through which many job printers prospered. The package usually sold for twenty-five cents and the profit may be indicated by the claims of some of the dealers that their agents could make as much as ten dollars a day. Soon the printers began adding things to their packages of stationery and called them "prize packages." Mysterious and alluring names were invented. One called his package the "Multi-microon" and another was entitled the "Panphrophosium." Whatever those resounding words were intended to mean has been lost to history, but certainly jawbreaking words were necessary to describe the contents of the packages bought so eagerly by a novelty hungry public. A typical offering was as follows:

Commercial Travelers and Agents wanted
to sell our 25 cent portfolio package

contents 18 sheets note paper, 18 envelopes, 1 pen holder, 1 pen, 1 pencil, 1 blotting pad, 100 recipes, 1 war hymn, 5 engravings, 1 new method of computing interest, 2 fashionable embroidery designs for collars, 4 for undersleeves, 2 for underskirts, 1 for corner of handkerchief, 2 for cuffs, 1 for silk purse, 1 for child's sack, 1 for ornamental pillow case, 1 puzzle garden and one beautiful article of jewelry. $10 a day can be realized. Send stamp for circular of wholesale prices.

WEIR & CO., 43 South Third Street, Philadelphia.

But the end had not yet been reached. Someone conceived the idea of making a shallow wooden box with a hinged lid which could be called a desk because the top did present a surface that was large enough to hold a sheet of paper. Desks were now offered, ready stocked with stationery! One enterprising man in Syracuse included a checker board and set of checkers.

Chapter X

CLOTHING FOR DEMOCRACY

MOST American industries which have since grown great were of humble origin, but they were respectable. This could not be said of the ready-made clothing business which wasn't started by manufacturers of clothing but by second-hand dealers. The business which is now so large and prosperous had its birth in dark water-front cellars where piles of dirty, worn, and patched garments and old hats, caps, and shoes were stored to be sold to sailors. The men who went to sea were the only customers of clothing shops. Less venturesome men who stayed at home had wives who could not only spin and weave but also sew, and who managed to whittle out some kind of clothing for the men of the family. The more prosperous employed professional tailors who kept an eye on returning travelers to note the style trends of Europe and England. Men of the sea enjoyed neither wives nor prosperity, but when they returned from long voyages they were in great need of clothing. And so the business of supplying men with coats and shirts and pants which were ready to wear was started as a kind of guttersnipe vocation rubbing shoulders with the crimps, pimps, and others who fattened on the hard-won earnings of the sailors. So deeply was the industry steeped in vice and iniquity that its reform was the work of a century.

No business started with less selling effort. When Jack came ashore he was often in rags but had wage money coming to him. This combination of an eager customer with cash in hand provided the ideal combination for a brisk and profitable trade. The only selling problem was that of getting Jack into the shop before the women and the grogshop took his money. The rest was easy and the percentage of profit was enormous. As a result of these profits, some of the New York shops later became respectable, abandoned the sailor trade, and moved uptown to cater to the smart college student trade. In their gentlemanly salesmen of today there is no trace of the predecessors who sold filthy rags to drunken sailors.

The principal problem was to keep a stock of goods on hand. This would not have been possible but for the fact that the homespun garments of a century and a half ago wore like iron and even after years of service were useful and saleable. Widows did not give a deceased husband's clothing to what then may have been the equivalent of the Salvation Army. It was thriftily sold. The dealers explored every avenue of supply. Peddlers traveling through the country were always willing to trade a few spools of thread or a dozen brass buttons for any old coat or shirt or pair of trousers or shoes. No matter how decrepit the garment might be, the dealers would pay for it, patch it up and make a saleable piece of merchandise out of it. Discarded military uniforms provided a staple article of trade.

The clothing shops centered around the seaports, Boston New York, Salem, Massachusetts, and Providence, Rhode Island. As the whaling business grew, New Bedford, Massachusetts, became the most important clothing city in the country. With more American ships being launched and a constantly increasing number of men sailing in them to distant ports of the world, the demand for "slops," as they were appropriately termed, became greater than the supply. Since there were not enough second-hand garments to meet the demands of the trade, the dealers reluctantly went into the manufacturing business. This meant that instead of making a quick and profitable turnover on a small stock of goods, they would have to make fairly large investments and wait a long time for returns. And so the ready-made clothing business was born. Its founders had no idea of building good will for their product. Their sales were made to customers who were in port today and gone tomorrow and would probably never be seen again. Under such circumstances any money spent on producing a quality article was just so much money wasted. So the dealers bought defective cloth, hired cheap tailors to cut it into patterns, and farmed out the making in a kind of crude sweatshop method—though most of the work was done in farm homes. They paid as little as possible for the work, held up payments or didn't pay at all if they could avoid it.

Jack was worse served than before. Under the old system the clothing he bought was second-hand and it might be covered with patches, but there was integrity in the fabric. It was either homespun or good honest cloth imported from England or Holland. The new clothing, however, possessed none of these characteristics. The dealer not only bought cloth of the poorest quality but encouraged spinners and weavers to produce even meaner cloth, providing always that it could be bought at a cheap price. The process of shrinking was neglected or omitted entirely, with the result that the purchaser, after he got out to sea, often found that he couldn't get into his clothing. Elbows came through sleeves in a little time and pants legs were ragged.

In the meantime selling methods operated under a greater head of steam. The amount invested in a stock of second-hand clothing was small and there was a quick turnover.

In the manufacturing venture large stocks of cloth had to be bought for cash and sent out to the country for making. The wait between the original investment and the sale was a matter of months, and the customer had to pay for it. All sales were made on the theory, which was a sound one, that he would be out at sea when the defects in the clothing began to appear and that he would never be seen again. It was on these principles of chicanery, deceit, and double-dealing that the great American clothing industry was founded.

While the making of suits of clothing was developing in this way, a young housewife in Troy, New York, unwittingly brought about a revolution in the construction of men's shirts. As a result, the shirt and collar business developed in what was, by comparison, an atmosphere of sweetness and light. About 1820 Mrs. Hannah Lord Montague of Troy, confronted with the unpleasant routine of wash day, noted that while the collar of one of her husband's shirts was dirty, the rest of the garment was clean. As she disliked washing but liked to sew, Mrs. Montague snipped the collar from the shirt, washed and ironed it, and then sewed it back on again. The result was entirely satisfactory. Other housewives who shared Mrs. Lord's aversion to the washtub adopted the same expedient and soon what had been started by a woman's whim changed the shirt styles of the world and created a new industry. The next step was to devise a method of tying the collar on with strings, and this was later followed by using the now familiar pair of collar buttons. Within a few years many Troy housewives had quit making collars on their husband's shirts and some of the stores were selling separate collars. The business which started in this casual way grew to its present production of millions of collars annually.

The production of collars, shirts, and the manufacture

of separate cuffs soon followed. The shirt without collar or cuffs could be made in much less time than the older style. Laundry work was simplified and the housewives' hours of labor lessened. More important eventually was the fact that collarless and cuffless shirts and separate collars and cuffs lent themselves to mass production. The full benefit of this was not realized until the perfection of the sewing machine. When the factories at Troy began producing better shirts than a housewife could make, and at a lower cost, shirt-making definitely and finally passed out of the constantly dwindling list of drudgeries known as household industries. A hundred years before this, the growing of flax, its process-ing, spinning, weaving, and the other work necessary for the production of a shirt required something like two weeks of work. Now a man could buy a shirt with the money he earned in one day's work. Life was rapidly getting easier, simpler, more comfortable.

Mrs. Montague's "invention" came at an opportune time. In colonial days a gentleman's shirt was made without a col-lar. The neck was covered with a stock or neck cloth, the breast with a ruff much like a ladies' shirtwaist front of forty years ago. In theory the neckpiece and ruff were always of spotless white—immaculate, usually the only piece of cloth-ing that could be called clean. In 1820 some of these old-fashioned costumes were still being worn, but the growing fashion was for shirts with collars attached, which meant that the whole garment had to be washed. As Horace Greeley later pontificated:

"It is evident that the daily emergencies of life should soil more rapidly the white surfaces exposed to the outer atmos-phere than those which are covered; and this is sufficient reason for putting on a clean collar and clean cuffs oftener than a clean shirt. There are no authentic statistics of shirts, so far as our present knowledge extends, but it requires no very complicated calculation to show that the number of collars and cuffs which must be manufactured in the United States must be immense."

With separate collars which could be easily washed, men became more conscious than ever of the cleanliness or lack of cleanliness in their neckwear. They demanded a gleaming white unwrinkled surface very difficult for the most skillful laundress to achieve. The result was a vogue for collars made of steel; enameled white, to be followed later by paper collars which held the stage for twenty years and then passed out of existence. The celluloid collar lasted well into the present century.

While the collar and cuff business as well as the making of shirts developed along healthy and wholesome lines, the business of making clothing for men pursued its wicked course and grew in volume through no virtues of its own. However, a new class of customer appeared on the scene— customers who did not sail away to distant ports as soon as they had made a purchase. With the development of factories, small as they were, there was a new demand for men's clothing that could be bought over the counter or handed down from a shelf. In the days of exclusive sailor trade this clothing had been known as "reach-me-downs," but for some reason the "hand-me-down" superseded it and got into the dictionaries shortly after the Civil War. The new customers consisted of young men from the farms who went to work in the factories in cities where they needed not only work clothes but suits for Sunday wear.

For the first time respectable bachelor trade became of some importance. The manufacturers of ready-made clothing were facing a period of great development but they did not know it. Looms and then spinning wheels were disappearing from the farms and a newer generation of housewives not only did not know how to spin or weave but refused to take the responsibility of doing the family tailoring. The demand for clothing continued to be greater than the supply, which made it easy for the manufacturers to sell merchandise of atrocious quality. The dealers had to be a little more careful and a little more plausible now that they had a class of customers who were permanent residents, but the basic technique of merchandising remained unchanged. A great deal of the ready-made clothing was imported, but it was little if any better than that locally produced.

While there was a slight change in merchandising methods, the clothing business was just as crooked as it had been when confined to cellar shops on the waterfront. But second-hand clothing supplied less and less of the sailor trade partly because the demand was so great and partly because when homespuns were replaced by poorer fabrics a second-hand suit was of no value. About 1825 the spinners and weavers thought up a new process and shoddy came on the market. Woolen rags and woolen clothing which were battered beyond repair were shredded, mixed with new wool, spun and woven into cloth. It looked like wool and actually was wool. But in the process of shredding the woolen fibers were broken so that a shoddy suit soon wore out. So many wore out earlier than expected, so many customers were deceived that the word which was a textile term of obscure origin became a very expressive adjective. With a good deal of justification, no one trusted a clothing merchant. Men who were fussy about their clothing became, or affected to be, textile experts who could by feeling, smelling, and tasting tell pure wool from shoddy.

Veteran clothing merchants looked back regretfully to the good old days when a customer walked out of the door never to be seen again. They knew that when the customer lived in the same town, the chances were that he would soon be back with complaints. A trade trick they adopted was to anticipate the event by a show of generosity. After the sale was made and the money paid over, the customer would be given a hat, a cap, a necktie, or a pair of suspenders. Another device—one still used in some country districts—was that of the peripatetic merchant who would rent a vacant store building, get rid of an assorted stock of goods in a hurry-up bargain sale, and then move on to some other county before the clothing he had sold began to disintegrate.

The clothing business remained disreputable while other lines of retail trade reformed and became honest because, as Franklin had said a hundred years earlier, "Honesty is the best policy." The famous A. T. Stewart, who made one of the early retailing fortunes by establishing a one-price policy, advertised in his great New York store that he sold "everything but men's and boys' ready-made clothing." He wouldn't risk his reputation on the class of merchandise he knew he would get.

Overcoats were the first garments to be honestly made. The manufacturers were not attempting to compete with what was known as the "Cheap John" trade but with the merchant tailors. It was much easier to find a fit in an overcoat than in a suit of coat, pants, and vest. A comparatively few sizes would meet the demands of almost everyone and it was not necessary to cut up a variety of fabrics. At first all the coats were made of the conventional black with a black velvet collar. This had always been the color for a gentle-man's clothing, a funereal garb accented by that atrocity, the black silk waistcoat. The overcoat manufacturers, once they they had become well established, ventured into plaids and checks and stripes, and for the first time American men did not appear like a nation of pallbearers. The new designs captured the fancy of the public. The first manifestation of this was the casting off of the old silk waistcoat; but this was replaced by fancy waistcoats even more atrocious. Some well-to-do dandies, who were later known as "dudes," often possessed a dozen or more of them, embracing a wide assortment of designs and colors.

The invention of the sewing machine gave the ready-made clothing business a boost by greatly reducing the cost of labor. It was made a practical machine just in time to be of great value in providing shoes and uniforms for the million soldiers of the Union army. Many of the clothing manufacturers made fortunes from army contracts, and they also learned something about the technique of mass production. After the war there was a steady demand for uniforms by fraternal organizations. The clothing manufacturers now had the technical skills and the mechanical equipment they needed.

It remained for John Wanamaker, Sunday School teacher, to make the clothing business respectable and so set up ethical standards which made possible the development of one of our great industries. He didn't undertake this until he had made one attempt in his new Philadelphia store to sell the shoddy goods which were typical of the period. The suits he offered for sale must have been just about the poorest the sweatshops could turn out, for the advertised price was $3.50. He had bought them cheap from a manufacturer in the panicky days following the outbreak of the Civil War. The venture had unpleasant consequences and this was his first and only experience with undependable merchandise. As soon as the lot of cheap suits was sold he adopted a new policy.

He boldly ordered the manufacture of suits to be made from pure wool, and bought the cloth himself to make sure of the quality. Other suits were made with different mixtures of wool, but each was distinctly and honestly marked. The suits naturally cost a great deal more than anyone had ever dreamed of paying for a ready-made. But for the first time the American who could not afford to pay the price demanded by the fashionable custom tailors was able to buy a suit made of honest cloth.

Wanamaker never talked about Christian principles in connection with merchandising. He sold dependable merchandise at cheap prices because it was profitable to do so. He probably never thought of himself as an apostle of practical democracy; but by bringing good clothing within a lower price bracket he leveled out inequalities that had enabled some men to appear much better dressed than others. His policy was such a success that in 1874 he had the largest retail business in the United States, although he sold nothing but men's and boys' clothing and furnishings.

The fact that he succeeded through selling clothing of honest quality led many others to follow his example. The initiative for quality merchandise came from the retail merchants, and for a long time the maintenance of this standard was also their responsibility. It was not until after Wanamaker and others had proved that it was profitable to sell clothing of quality that manufacturers fell in line. They produced clothing of established quality and marked it with

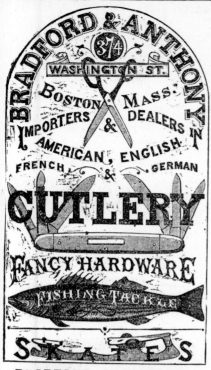

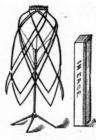

Mrs. Loudon made papier mache busts for San Francisco ladies

The Treasure Belt made life difficult for pickpockets

ABOVE IS AN OUTLINE SKETCH OF A BEAUTIFUL PERFUMED CARD ADVERTISING **HOYT'S GERMAN COLOGNE,** THE MOST FRAGRANT AND LASTING OF PERFUMES.
THIS COLOGNE IS SOLD BY ALL DEALERS. PRICE 25 CENTS, 50 CENTS, AND $1.00 PER BOTTLE.
NEVER IN A 10 CENT SIZE. BEWARE OF CHEAP IMITATIONS.

E. W. HOYT & CO., SOLE MANUFACTURERS, LOWELL, MASS.

SEND 2 CENT STAMP FOR PERFUMED CARDS.

TRY **RUBIFOAM,** OUR NEW LIQUID DENTIFRICE. DELICIOUSLY FLAVORED. HARMLESS.
ELEGANTLY PUT UP. 25 CENTS PER BOTTLE.

JUST HIS LUCK.

"Did her father actually thrust you off the stoop, Mr. Noodle?" said the lawyer.

"Yes, sir. It broke my heart."

"Well, you have my sympathy. If he had broken your leg instead of your heart, you could have sued him. *SOME MEN NEVER HAVE ANY LUCK.*"

But when a man finds the most **Stylish, Comfortable, and Serviceable Shoe** for only **$3.00** he has the **good luck** which attends all that wear the

GEO. A. DENHAM

IMPROVED $3.00 SHOE.
(Smooth Inner Sole).

If you cannot get this make of Shoes from your dealer. send for directions how to procure them.

GEO. A. DENHAM, 125 Federal Street, Boston, Mass.

"NEW" *Langtry* REG'D

PARIS SHAPE.

Latest Paris Fashion Magazines indicate that, instead of less, more of a bustle is to be worn this year. The Paris bustle has more shelf than formerly, to support the drapery, and our latest LANGTRY is modelled after this last Paris style. Be sure to ask for the LANGTRY.

For sale at all leading Dry-Goods Houses.

PRICE, PER MAIL, 60 CENTS.

Patented in U. S., Canada, and Europe.

THE CANFIELD RUBBER CO.,
86 Leonard Street., New York.

The Langtry Bustle was a bargain at sixty cents

BUSINESS MEN, ATTENTION.

The United States Life Insurance Company, having recently re-organized its Agency Department in this city, is now prepared to negotiate with competent and successful business men who feel disposed to engage in soliciting for life insurance in this city and vicinity, as a permanent business.

Bear in mind that the Company is desirous of making engagements with men strictly new to the business, whose past record will warrant a trial in this field.

Come one and all and talk the matter over.

John E. De Witt,
President,
261 Broadway.

The Daily Graphic has achieved the most Brilliant Success It is to-day More Widely Read than Any Other Evening Paper in New York.

Seven Steam Presses, aided by the most extensive Machinery, have been wholly inadequate to supply the demand. The Daily Graphic is read by

75.000

People Daily.

As a Newspaper, it is more popular than any other Evening Paper in New York. As an Advertising medium, it Gives More for the money than Any Other Paper.

Good as it was, the Daily Graphic didn't last long

People gave rocking chairs as Christmas presents in 1878

Stove polish was a household necessity

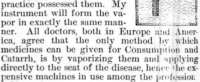

their brand names. Before that time the merchant had to be an expert in manufacturing and watch carefully every bale of merchandise brought into his shop. When the manufacturers began making goods under their own brand names and assumed this responsibility themselves, the cost of distribution dropped. The Wanamaker name was one of the first, if not the first, to appear on the label of a suit of ready-made clothing, but now there are dozens of names, each of which stands as a guarantee of dependable quality.

The cheap prices for good clothing have eliminated the visual distinction of class which are so apparent in cities of other countries. Here and here only, nine-tenths of the men are well dressed in clothing of such uniform appearance that bank clerk and bank president appear the same.

Chapter XI

THE PEOPLE LEARN THE NEWS

IN THE first half of the last century, a little more than a hundred years ago, the demand for reading matter in New York as well as in other American cities was much greater than the supply. Nothing else will explain the fact that about 1830 the city provided a total of approximately twenty-six thousand five hundred subscribers to the seven morning and four afternoon dailies which had been established long enough to be looked on as permanent institutions. From this remote and detached point of view it appears that if there had been anything else to read, these papers could not have existed. It is difficult to understand what curious demand for reading matter they may have satisfied. The sorriest and most unprogressive country weekly of today contains more of interest than could be found in any of these metropolitan journals. Rarely did any issue of any one of them contain as much as three columns of reading matter and more than three-fourths of the space was taken up with "cards" of merchants and other business houses. Some sprightly New York matron who found nothing of interest in her husband's paper is said to have remarked on the fortunate coincidence that the pages fit the pantry shelves.

There were no date lines, no reporters, no despatches except those reprinted from London and other foreign newspapers at a decent interval after the trans-Atlantic mails arrived. Editors sat in their sanctums and gave written expression to pontifical opinions on ponderous subjects, occasionally writing slanderous articles about editors of competing papers. The most exciting news they ever published was about the assaults that editors made on each other. A horsewhip was the favorite weapon. When loafers saw an editor with fire in his eye walking about the streets with a horsewhip, they followed him in the certainty that there would be a good show as soon as he found the man he was looking for—more fun than a dog fight. As the editor was the puppet of some political party and party passions were violent, there were many provocations to violence. A fairly steady diet was provided of abuse of political parties with which the editor did not agree.

The subscribers for these poorly printed and poorly edited sheets paid six cents a copy for them. Considered in terms of purchasing power, six cents would be the equivalent today of more than twenty-five cents. Up in Connecticut farmers were providing bed, board, and clothing to the county poor for a dollar a week. A Staten Island boarding school was advertising for pupils at $25.00 a quarter and glad to get them at that price which left a comfortable profit for the school proprietor. More than half a century was to elapse before the nickel could be looked upon as a coin small enough for casual spending.

The town was full of lively and important news which the diligent reader could sometimes discover in these stodgy sheets, usually after he had heard about it from other sources. The State Legislature had allowed New Yorkers to elect their own mayor. Tammany had been organized to control the votes of the newly arrived Irish immigrants. But the only people who could keep themselves informed as to the views of the opinion-molding editors were those who could afford to pay what was a very high price for a daily

paper. It was in accordance with the best journalistic practice to edit newspapers for the upper classes and price them
accordingly. In 1815 the great *London Times* had sold for
seven pence a copy and enjoyed a circulation of five thousand. That was in the year of Waterloo when presumably
every Londoner who could afford it would have bought a
morning paper to see whether or not the British Empire was
still in existence. Later the *Times* brought the price down
to three pence and in 1830 had a staggering circulation of
seventeen thousand. That was probably the reason the New
York papers fixed their price at six cents. The *Times* was
the world's one great newspaper and all editors tried to
emulate it in every way.

There were no indications of it in the stodgy papers of
New York and the other cities, but democratic journalism
was on its way. Throughout the country a great many printers, who worked at the cases putting into type the ponderous
opinions of the editors, dreamed of starting papers of their
own—papers which could be bought and read by men of
their own income class to whom six cents meant the price of
a meal. They thought they could sell more papers and make
more money at one cent a copy, just as Terry had believed
he could make more money by selling a cheaper clock. Several "penny papers" started in Boston and Philadelphia
had flourished brilliantly for a time and then had failed.

The venture had been undertaken in the wrong towns.
Boston and Philadelphia were rich and conservative, with a
very large proportion of the class we now call intelligentsia.
New York had the largest population in the country but not
many of its residents were wealthy. It certainly had more
people than any other city who could not afford to pay six
cents for a paper but could afford to pay one cent. That was

the constant theme of conversation of David Ramsey who with more than a dozen other compositors worked at the type cases of the *Journal of Commerce*. One of the compositors was Benjamin H. Day, who talked less but worked harder than Ramsey. He saved his money and after a few years of work quit his job to start a printing business at a very inopportune moment. The cholera epidemic had killed more than thirty thousand people in New York in 1832 and the job printing business, like every other business in town, had been hard hit.

While Day waited for customers, the arguments of Ramsey about the money to be made in a one-cent paper kept recurring to him. As the job printing business continued to languish, Day, with very little preparation or help, launched the *Daily Sun*, price one cent per copy, on September 3, 1833. If he knew that this was the fiftieth anniversary of the signing of the peace treaty with England, he said nothing about it in this first issue.

Just a short time before this Horace Greeley, with a capital of one hundred and fifty dollars, had started a paper to sell for one cent but it had failed after just three weeks. Day had little if any more cash than Greeley, but the mechanical cost of printing his little paper was small, and the editorial expense practically nothing. Besides he had some income from the job printing business, and he hoped the paper would bring him more job printing even if it was not a money-maker in itself.

Greeley was only twenty-two years old when he started his paper and Day was only one year older when he launched the *Sun*. But Day was married and living with his wife and infant son in Duane Street, only a few blocks from the newspaper office. To the other young printers in New York

Greeley was a highbrow who would argue with William Cullen Bryant, the distinguished editor of the *Post*. Day looked on himself as a practical businessman, had no ideas about reforming the world or making anyone else agree with him on political issues. To him the publication of the *Sun* was a business enterprise which should be profitable, just like the printing of circulars. Other papers had been launched with flamboyant and highly oratorical statements of ideals and purposes, but printer Day's announcement in the first issue of the *Sun* was very simple and businesslike:

"The object of this paper is to bring before the public, at a price within the means of everyone, all the news of the day, and at the same time afford an advantageous means for advertising."

After working all night on the first issue Day put the paper to bed and went to bed himself. He had been too busy to collect any news for the paper which had promised to tell all the news. But at the last moment he bought one of the six cent papers, which had gone to press earlier, re-wrote some of the news it contained and set the type for it himself. It was not by any means all the news, but it was all he had been able to get.

The first edition of a thousand copies or less was sold out during the morning and, although Day himself did not know it, newspapers for the masses were on the way. Day not only hired a reporter or two but introduced another inno-vation by sending newsboys out to sell the paper on the streets. Within two years from the time it was started the *Sun* had a circulation of nineteen thousand exceeding that of the *London Times* by two thousand. A few years later in 1836 the circulation was twenty-seven thousand, the largest circulation of any daily paper in the world. Penny journalism had succeeded. The highly respectable six cent papers which had been read only by the wealthy struggled on, but they fought a losing fight. One by one they lowered their prices or passed out of existence. The cheap paper sold more copies; the publisher made more money, and therefore could spend more for news and on the salaries of editors, and thus produce a better paper. It was only a few decades after the first copy of the little four-page *Sun* appeared on the streets before there were more per capita readers of newspapers in the United States than in any other country in the world. That has continued to be true. We have always had, population considered, more newspapers, more readers, and more thorough news coverage than any other people.*

With the readers of a newspaper numbering tens of thousands, advertising began to play an important part in business, a part that was to continue to grow in importance until it became essential to the interdependent machinery of mass production and mass merchandising. Its first use was by retail merchants. They found that by advertising their goods they could attract more customers, make a quicker turnover of their stock and so make a greater profit on the money invested. As they could double or triple or quadruple the pulling power of the advertisement by the offer of lower prices, it came about quite naturally that the benefits of this economy in the cost of selling were passed on, in part at least, to the customer in the form of lower prices.

However, the effective use of advertising was not an immediate development. During the first generation of daily newspapers in New York there were few indications of the

* (It has often been said that a French newspaper was the first to achieve a circulation of a million copies daily and there have been spectacular figures regarding the circulation of newspapers in Japan. In both cases these figures are due to the exaggerated claims of publishers.)

part that advertising was destined to play. The publishers as well as the advertisers were only vaguely conscious of the functions of advertising. The copy appearing in all papers consisted of musty cards which ran month after month and year after year without any changes. Advertisers generally thought that if they kept their names before the public the function of advertising had been completely fulfilled. The newspaper card was nothing more than an extension of the sign in front of the shop. It was not at all unusual for fur overcoats and Christmas toys to be advertised in July. The only advertisements that were kept up-to-date and were of any practical value to the advertiser or usefulness to the public were the shipping announcements. These cards, giving dates of sailings, quite appropriately had the place of honor on the front page top of the first column. Indeed about the only function performed by advertising was to add to the bulk of the papers. Rarely did the reading matter in an entire issue of the *Herald, Sun, Post* or any other paper amount to as much as is contained in a single page of a standard sized newspaper of today. It could all have been printed on a single sheet, but the papers all consisted of four pages. In 1840, when its success had been assured, more than twenty of the twenty-eight colums of the *Sun* consisted of advertising.

No publisher bothered with anything less than an annual contract for fixed advertising space and the standard space measurement was the "square," which meant a space equal in depth to the width of a column—approximately two column inches. The rate for this space was pretty well standardized at thirty dollars a year, which worked out at about two cents a column inch. But with "casual advertisements" it was a different story. No one published any rates for this kind of business but announced ambiguously: "Casual advertisements at usual rates." This in many cases meant whatever the advertiser could be induced to pay. Certainly the employer who advertised offering a reward for the return of a runaway apprentice boy or the merchant who announced the arrival of a new cargo of merchandise from England had to pay a great deal more than two cents a column inch. These advertisements were worth more because they contained real news, were read and produced results. The publishers did not charge a higher rate because of this, however, but because of the time it took to put the advertisement into type and place it in the columns. They had no conception of the value of the space they were selling, but a later generation learned it.

James Gordon Bennett perhaps unwittingly made advertising an invaluable aid to selling when he founded the *Herald* in 1835. He made no annual contracts for "cards" to be paid for in advance. This procedure, which had been followed by all other publishers who started newspapers, provided a convenient method of securing working capital. Contracts for fifty cards at thirty dollars each, paid for in advance, would bring in fifteen hundred dollars which was just three times the amount of money Bennett had with which to start his paper.

Day was the first editor to realize that newspaper readers wanted news rather than political arguments, Bennett the first to realize that advertising may be news. He was determined that the columns of his paper should not be cluttered with the dead weight of dull business cards, and he took stern precautions to prevent it. He announced that all advertising published in the *Herald* would, in effect, be casual; that it would be published for only two weeks. If through carelessness an advertisement were published for a longer period, no charge would be made for the extra space used. One reason for this policy was that he wanted plenty of space for his news, space which he was soon going to need. Perhaps also his thrifty Scotch soul revolted at the thought of the columns filled with cards which were of little conceivable value to the advertisers. Also, he may not have been unconscious of the fact that there was more revenue in a single column of casual advertisements than in a whole page of cards.

The new policy which had been derided by the other publishers was a success. The *Herald's* advertising columns were slim but profitable not only to the publisher but also to the advertisers. People read them because they were interesting and they brought results. The plan worked so well that on January 1, 1848, Bennett announced a new and even more startling rule. No advertisement was to be accepted for more than a single insertion, which was to be paid for in cash in advance. He established a flat rate for advertising with no space discounts so that the small advertiser bought space at the same rate as the large. The rate was approximately twenty-five cents per column inch.

These were reforms in advertising policy which were bound to come, but Bennett anticipated a development which might have been delayed for years. Other publishers followed the *Herald's* policy and with increasing circulations the advertising columns of newspapers became an indispensable factor in the economical distribution of goods. John Wanamaker, pioneer in many things, was the man who started department store advertising. He published the first half-page advertisement in 1877 and the first full page five years later.

Having learned the simple lesson that their readers wanted the news, American publishers used every conceivable device and stratagem to get it for them. For some time the most important news came from Europe, brought here by ships before the laying of the Atlantic cable. Publishers in Boston and New York bought small swift yachts which would meet ships beyond the quarantine station and sail back with the late copies of European papers. Some papers covered long distances with relays of horses and riders. The most famous of these was maintained by the Baltimore *Sun* during the war with Mexico. Sixty riders of fast horses covered the route from the Mexican border to Baltimore bringing despatches from the front which were usually several days in advance of the news received by the War Department.

The speeches of Daniel Webster always provided big news, and the papers vied with each other to be the first to publish them. Henry J. Raymond, a famous New York reporter, made a notable beat on one occasion when Webster made an important speech in Boston. Raymond went there with a staff of compositors and an equipment of type cases, which were set up on a boat scheduled to sail for New York soon after the conclusion of the speech. On the way from Boston to New York Raymond transcribed his notes and wrote his story which the printer put into type. When the boat arrived in New York the galleys were ready to be put into the forms and sent to press. Thanks to these energetic methods, the number of newspaper readers grew until between 1840 and 1850 New York, with a much smaller population, was buying more papers than London.

The building of telegraph lines followed by the laying of the Atlantic cable provided the newspapers with new opportunities for the swift transmission of news. But the telegraph rates were high and advertising revenue was small and the papers could make but sparing use of this new facility. In 1860, when Lincoln was nominated for the presidency, a single telegraph operator at the convention was able to handle all the press messages offered. In 1892, when Cleveland was nominated, the Western Union alone kept one hundred operators busy and there were many leased wires. Cable and telegraph rates had gone down and advertising revenue had greatly increased. In 1870 a Boston Sunday paper had such a glut of advertising that it was compelled to increase its size from four to eight pages, which brought out strong protests from old subscribers. A few years later people were talking about the huge twenty-four page papers published in New York. The Sunday newspapers with news, entertainment, and a variety of features on many subjects is the greatest bargain one can buy today, for its production may have cost several hundred thousand dollars. But Americans have never quit complaining about the size of these papers, while they are, of course, simply staggering to British and European visitors.

With the growth of revenue from circulation and advertising, publishers spent money more and more lavishly. One of the most sensational expenditures was made by the Chicago *Times* in 1881. The work of the revision of the English translation of the Bible had been begun ten years before this and was participated in by a large number of American scholars, although the committee meetings were all held in England. When the revised version of the New Testament was finally approved the *Times* had eight thousand words of the text cabled to Chicago. This must have been considered a successful venture in spite of its cost, for when the complete text reached New York by steamer it was telegraphed to the *Times*. More than twenty operators were required. Undoubtedly this feat, which was the journalistic sensation of the day, provided the background for the many exaggerated stories about newspaper correspondents filing the Bible in order to hold the cable or telegraph line while an important story was being written.

From the time that Day's one cent *Sun* was started American publishers have constantly demanded better printing equipment, and for a long time the circulation of the more popular papers was limited by the number of papers the presses could print. About the time of the Civil War the New York *Tribune* made stereotypes of the type forms so that two or more presses could be used on the same issue. Before that time newspapers with big circulations worked against a vicious handicap. They had to go to press earlier than their smaller rivals and thus were often beaten on important news.

As department store advertising brought increasing revenue to the publishers, some of the more astute were impressed by the fact that while American men earn the money, the women spend it. Therefore if department store advertising was to be profitable to the advertiser, it was essential that the newspapers have women readers. In the early days of New York journalism a matron had commented that the papers were only good for the lining of pantry shelves. Today every paper pays a great deal of attention to the problems of its women readers. In the course of a year she will get in her daily paper more recipes than can be found in the fattest cookbook, in addition to well considered advice on every subject of possible feminine interest, from the polishing of fingernails to the weaning of babies.

Day, Greeley, Bennett, and practically all the other men who founded newspapers in America were poor men who started with a very small amount of capital. In hundreds of communities the first newspaper was started by a printer who had, as the saying goes, "nothing but a press and a shirt tail full of type." Many of these papers founded in such an humble way are now worth millions of dollars. But they have never lost the democratic tradition. Most of them are independent of party politics except where there is in effect only one party. Some may support the claims of capital and others the claims of labor, but the success of each depends on the volume of circulation it can maintain—and volume cannot be secured from any one class or sect or party. No matter how wealthy a newspaper proprietor may be, he must continue to produce what is essentially a democratic piece of merchandise.

Chapter XII

THE ROAD TO THE CONSUMER

RAILWAY, bus, steamship, and airplane lines now cover our country with a network of transportation that brings every part of it into easy and convenient access with every other. Freight rates are so cheap that the products of any state can, with a few minor exceptions, be sold in any other state. The physical isolation of the colonial period has disappeared and the only remaining institutions that were brought into being by that isolation are the distilleries which produce rye and bourbon whiskey. These unique American beverages were first produced on North American soil, and are today produced in no other part of the world. They might never have been made here if people living in the interior of the country had not been so isolated from the seaports that they could not sell their grain and buy rum which was imported in such large quantities from Jamaica and other sugar-producing islands. Pioneer Americans were rum drinkers but rum was to be had only at seaports and when settlers occupied land far in the interior they were cut off from their favorite tipple.

In fairness to the hardy pioneers whose corn and rye went into the making of whiskey, it should be pointed out that this development came about not alone through a desire for strong drink but also because of the need to find a market for the product of their farms. Good crops in Western Pennsylvania, Kentucky, and Ohio did not necessarily bring prosperity. In places where everyone was raising corn, there was no market for surplus crops, for everyone had all that he needed. The only places where corn could be sold were in the distant ports and it cost more to haul the corn there than the corn was worth. In many instances the journey was so long that a horse would have to eat all the corn he could carry before he could get to his destination. But corn made into whiskey was a product occupying such a small amount of space and selling at such a high price that it could be transported long distances at a profit. As a result, corn was sent to market in the form of whiskey, the only way in which it could be sold with anything like a fair profit to the farmer. In some places in Ohio where there were no local distilleries, corn was sold on some occasions at ten cents a bushel, less than one-seventh of the market price at seaboard towns.

The arrangement with the distiller was a very simple one. He traded one gallon of whiskey for one bushel of corn, a convenient arrangement which finally became an established trade custom. It was satisfactory to the farmer, and equally satisfactory to the distiller who produced three gallons of whiskey from one bushel of corn. In this way whiskey became the farmers' money crop and in all corn-growing regions replaced rum as a popular tipple. This method of marketing corn was so important that when the national government in 1791 put an internal revenue tax of nine cents a gallon on whiskey, the farmers of the West rose in armed revolt. This "Whiskey Rebellion" was put down by United States troops but later all taxes were repealed. There was no tax on whiskey until 1862, when revenue was needed for the support of the Union army, and the building of railways had provided a means of getting corn and other farm products to market.

It is very interesting to note that the farmers in mountainous districts of China and Iran, where the production of opium has been the most persistent, suffer from a similar isolation. Markets are so distant from these opium-producing areas that there is no sale for food crops. But opium is so valuable and occupies such a small space that the product of a year's labor may be carried concealed in one's clothing. The result is that farmers in these areas grow only enough food for their own families and use the remainder of their land for growing the opium poppy.

As Americans thought of transportation in terms of boats, it was natural that first attention should be turned to the building of canals, and during the first half of last century there was an era of canal building which has been half forgotten. The early canals were not ambitious projects like the Erie which connected Buffalo with Albany, a distance of 340 miles. Most of them ran for only short distances providing a method of getting boats around rapids in an otherwise navigable river. Many of the canals that were constructed were abandoned soon after the railway came in and those which are still in operation no longer play the important roles they did in the past. One defect in canal transportation which doomed it from the beginning was the fact that canals froze over in winter time and so enjoyed only a seasonal usefulness. At the time they were projected this did not appear to be of supreme importance, as the principal reason for them was to provide a cheap method of getting crops to market. But as developing industries gathered speed and momentum, delays of this sort could not be tolerated. The fact that the canal barges traveled only two miles an hour was not considered any serious handicap to this method of transportation.

For many years the trade of each state and each community

was very severely limited by the lack of transportation. For example, in the period before 1840 or 1850 a merchant who wanted to ship goods from any point in Virginia to any point in Ohio had to use a circuitous route covering hundreds of miles by land and water. After landing the goods in Richmond he would ship it down the James River and thence by ocean steamer to the Gulf of Mexico to New Orleans. Here the cargo would be transferred to another boat going up the Mississippi and Ohio Rivers and eventually reach Cincinnati, to be transshipped there by any means that was available.

Very few schedules of old freight rates are available, but the postage rates charged in 1842 provide a very illuminating index as to costs of transportation which would be considered prohibitive today. The cost of sending a letter to a local address was six cents, provided the distance was less than thirty miles. Charges increased with the distance until the rate for letters between Boston and New York or Philadelphia and New York was twenty-five cents. These rates applied on letters written on one sheet of foolscap paper, folded and sealed without an envelope. If the letter or invoice or legal document consisted of two sheets of paper, the rate was doubled; if of three sheets, it was tripled.

The charges fell very heavily on business concerns which carried on a regular daily correspondence with agents, and in spite of the fact that the carrying of mail was a government monopoly, there were many evasions of the law. If a man from New York was planning a business trip to either of these cities, he usually notified his friends in advance so that they could have their letters prepared for him to carry. This was a plain violation of the law, and there were some prosecutions. But these were usually unsuccessful, for it was difficult to convince a jury that a man who had done nothing more than carry some letters for friends was guilty of a misdemeanor. In spite of these high rates the post office in the year of 1842 carried no less than thirty million letters, a little less than two letters for each inhabitant of the country. The newspapers thought this was something to be proud of. There were more than thirteen thousand post offices and the postal route covered more than a hundred thousand miles.

Canals, steamboats, and railways all appeared at the same time to excite the public imagination, and bitter were the controversies and clashes of special interests. The powerful financial and political coterie which had backed Robert Fulton in his steamship enterprise tried to secure a monopoly on the steam navigation of all the rivers of the country— and almost succeeded. This group did not believe in railways and tried to prevent the building of any in New York state. Their spokesman predicted that many accidents would result when the heavy carriages rolled along at a speed of four miles an hour. The state engineer of Virginia said it was an admitted fact "that a rate of speed of more than six miles an hour would exceed the bounds set by prudence, though some of the sanguine advocates of railways extend this speed to nine miles an hour." These speeds were terrific when compared with the canal barge making two miles an hour which was also the approximate speed of a pack train.

An attempt was made to impose building restrictions which would make the building of railways so expensive as to be prohibitive. The spokesman for the steamship interests contended: "The walls on which they (the rails) are placed must be at least four feet below the surface, and three feet above, and must be clamped with iron, and even then would hardly sustain so heavy a weight as you propose moving at the rate of four miles an hour on wheels. . . . The means of stopping these heavy carriages without a great shock, and of preventing them from running upon each other (for there would be many on the road at once) would be very difficult. In case of accidental stops, or the necessary stops to take wood and water, etc. many accidents would happen."

Many other dire consequences were predicted. It was said that the smoke from the engines would poison the air so that wild birds and vegetation along the track would be killed. Hens would not lay, horses and cattle would starve. As a final sordid touch it was said that people would be driven insane by terror. An early doctor warned the people against railways saying, "the human body cannot stand such terrific speeds."

It was against this background of prejudice and superstition and powerful organized opposition that the railways of the country were built. Later, on more than one occasion, the sons of these early obstructionists opposed the extension of railways for an entirely different reason. The terminus of a railway line enjoyed unusual advantages for it automatically became the center of distribution for all the surrounding area. When it was proposed to push the line farther on, citizens of the terminal towns felt that their vested rights were being sacrificed, and they tried to prevent the extension by legal action and at times by mob violence.

People generally were skeptical about railways, just as their great-grandchildren were later skeptical about automobiles and a still later generation about the radio. Then, as later with the motorcars, skepticism was replaced by enthusiasm, and the whole country participated in discussions as to methods of building and operation. Many of the die-hards who were willing to concede that it was practical for horses to pull carriages over a pair of rails balked at the idea of using a steam engine. They lightly cast aside the fact that a steam railway was in successful operation in England. Many a rural economist disposed of the problem in a way that he thought to be completely unanswerable. He conceded that a steam railway might be a successful undertaking in England where coal was cheap and oats dear. But just the reverse was true in this country where oats were cheap and coal either dear or unobtainable. In 1827 this objection to a steam railway was incorporated in a Massachusetts legislative report and there was considerable support for a project to build a horse-drawn railroad from Boston to Albany. The Baltimore and Ohio Railway began by using horses attached to a single car and the directors considered the matter for some time before deciding to use steam.

But the general adoption of steam did not end the controversy in which the general public as well as the stockholders engaged. An unfortunate accident on one of the early roads prolonged discussion of the subject. A Negro slave who was firing the engine was annoyed by the steam coming from the safety valve and put a stop to it by leaning against the valve. The result was that the boiler blew up, wrecking the engine and killing the fireman. The fear of boiler explosions was so persistent that some of the early roads placed a car full of bales of cotton just to the rear of the engine. This was known as the "barrier car."

The early railways, like the early canals, were not complete transportation units in themselves. Like the canals they merely connected one sea- or river-port with another. The Baltimore and Ohio was promoted as an answer to the threat to Baltimore trade created by the building of the Erie Canal. The road, as the name indicates, was designed to connect the city with some port on the Ohio. Enthusiastic as the early railway partisans were, there were few of them who dreamed that the railway would ever be more than a feeder for the steamboats or the sailing ships. They certainly did not dream of a time when one would pay twice as much for transportation if it was twice as fast.

By the time the horse supporters had been defeated, the bitter controversy over routes was at white heat, and the rivalries of towns and villages engendered civic hatreds which persisted for generations. Adherents of either proposed route supported their plan with the violent oratory generally reserved for presidential elections; they made speeches, wrote letters to the newspapers. The technique of the political election was usually followed with more meetings, oratory and torchlight parades. Public-spirited men became amateur surveyors and singly or in groups made long journeys on horseback through forests they hoped would soon be traversed by the iron horses. Railway promoters were quick to exploit these rivalries, and a great many towns gave the companies large sums of money, raised by popular subscription, to influence the selection of the route.

The railways brought down the cost of transportation both of freight and passengers, and by providing a cheaper and more efficient method of distribution led to the development of many industries, the establishment of many factories. It didn't put an end to the distilling business, but did make it unnecessary for the farmer to trade his corn for whiskey.

The railroad business was something entirely new, demanding many highly specialized skills which had not yet been developed. The rails were wooden joists on which strips of iron were nailed. The equipment was poor and accidents frequent. Old files of *Harper's Weekly* with monotonous regularity depict many terrible things that happened to trains.

Their operation was considered such a hazardous vocation that engineers, firemen, brakemen, and conductors were denied policies by the life insurance companies. This led to the organization of the "brotherhoods," now powerful labor organizations but originally formed as benevolent organizations to provide members with insurance protection.

Both freight and passenger rates were high according to present-day ideas—not necessarily because they were monopolistic and beyond government control but because costs of operation were high. A ton of coal would pull but a fraction of the freight it pulls today. Engines were inefficient, tracks were poor and the loads carried by the heavy cars were light. Trains were slow and ran only in daylight, thus requiring the services of a great number of trainmen. Old schedules of both freight and passenger rates if applied today would bring the business of the country to a standstill.

In 1849 the passenger fare from Albany to Buffalo was twelve dollars. This provided accommodations beside which the most antiquated coach on the road today would appear luxurious. The car wheels were not cast in a single piece but constructed with spokes like a wagon wheel and the rattle was deafening. Windows as well as wheels rattled and had to be closed at all times as a protection against the shower of sparks from the wood-burning engine. Travel by train was much faster than by stagecoach but tediously slow for the nineteenth century. The train left Albany at nine o'clock in the morning and with only a few stops reached Auburn, a distance of 174 miles, thirteen hours later. Here passengers spent the night, resuming the journey at nine the next morning and reaching Buffalo about eleven o'clock at night. The fare by steamer from Buffalo to Detroit was eighteen dollars. As the equipment of railways was improved and the management became more efficient, the costs of operation were reduced and these reductions were passed on to the public in the form of reduced freight and passenger rates, though not very readily, it must be admitted.

High as they were, these rates were very much cheaper than those of stagecoaches and freight wagons. The building of railways brought about a general reduction in manufacturing costs because of cheaper transportation and a general improvement in quality of merchandise because small local monopolies were broken up and competition spread over a wider field. Before the coming of the railways the local manufacturer was limited to his own particular area but there he had a monopoly, for the cost of transportation made it impossible for manufacturers a hundred miles distant to compete with him. He was under no necessity to keep his price low or quality high. Towns were more charming and colorful when the local cigarmaker, blacksmith, baker, and harnessmaker were fixtures of the community, but we get better and cheaper food and merchandise now than our grandparents did.

With each year there was improvement in railway equipment and service, until in 1871 it looked as if the ultimate in travel comfort had been achieved with the building of the new sleeping cars. They were American in conception because they did not consist of rows of compartments. A newspaper man of that date pointed with pride to this American achievement, referring to the new car as "a democratic palace instead of a nest of aristocratic closets." There were many other manifestations of democracy. The first cars contained no bed clothes—only mattresses. Later, sheets and blankets were stored in a closet and passengers could help themselves and make their own beds. There was also a wash-basin and a towel in each car.

The building of railways did not bring cheap freight rates except in the sense that it was cheaper to ship by rail than to haul goods long distances by horse and wagon. Neither was freight on canal boats and river steamers cheap. In 1859, for example, the cost of shipping barrels of flour from Minneapolis to Boston was $2.25 per hundred pounds, a rate that would be prohibitive today.

Freight rates could not be materially reduced until the operation of railways was put on a more efficient basis; and they were not reduced until the railways stopped their rate cutting wars, in which some shippers were penalized for the benefit of others. The era of lower rates for both passengers and freight began about 1873. In 1893 the freight bill of the country was about eight hundred million dollars. Stuyvesant Fish, the leading railway executive of the period, calculated that if the rates of twenty years earlier had prevailed the charges would have been in excess of two billion dollars.

"Rates have fallen to a point absolutely impossible before the era of improvement," he said, "and both freight and passengers are now transported for less money, and with more safety, speed, and convenience than in any other country on the face of the earth."

One of the principal economies in the operation of railways was made possible by the general adoption of steel rails which about 1873 began to replace the old iron rails. This made it possible to pull heavier loads with the same traction power and reduced the wear and tear on rolling stock. This reduction in freight rates made possible by the use of steel rails provides an illuminating example of the way in which the American consumer benefits by every technological advance. Thousands of steel technicians working over a period of years finally produce a steel rail cheap enough to be used by the railways. This makes possible a reduction in freight rates. Thus food and manufactured articles find a wider distribution at a lower cost and everyone is benefited.

Chapter XIII

HONEST GOODS AT HONEST PRICES

IT DIDN'T just happen that about a hundred years ago the American retail merchant began to abandon selling policies which retailers had been following from the time the first retail shop was opened. The ancient policy was summed up in the Latin phrase *caveat emptor*, which is literally translated: "Let the buyer beware." As interpreted by the shopkeeper, this threw on the customers the entire responsibility for getting a dollar's worth of merchandise for each dollar that he spent. If the dealer gave honest weight and honest measure, he felt that he had fulfilled his obligation. It was the responsibility of the customer to see that he paid a fair price and got good quality. If he failed to do so that was his bad luck as had been decided by eminent jurists in a number of court cases, in many countries and over a period of centuries.

Even in the matter of honest measure not all of the merchants were overly punctilious, if we are to believe the popular story of the origin of the American phrase: "get down to brass tacks." As a convenient method of measuring cloth the merchant nailed brass-headed tacks on the dry goods counter showing a yard length. The salesman could easily measure the cloth while unrolling the bolt on the counter. But according to tradition they were in the habit of doing the measuring very swiftly, holding the cloth above the counter and in that way measuring some rather short yards. Hence the customer's demand that he get down to brass tacks. Perhaps the custom was not very common, but the phrase struck the popular fancy because of the general distrust of all merchants.

The only merchandise rule the early merchant knew—the only rule those who sold goods to their fellow men had ever known—was to buy cheaply and sell dearly. Adherence to that policy meant, it was thought, certain profits. Fixed prices were unknown. It was the custom to mark all articles with the price in plain figures while a code figure indicated either the actual cost price or the lowest possible selling price. PAY ME QUICK was a favorite code among country storekeepers as it was an easily remembered phrase containing ten unduplicated letters. The merchant always hoped to get the price marked in plain figures but if the customer was difficult there was leeway for some reduction which could be made without taking a loss.

An argument over price was the customary prelude to a sale of anything but the most trivial article. With the code figure alongside the marked selling price, the smart clerk had a distinct advantage over the customer. If the latter was easygoing, he might pay the marked price without question. On the other hand if he was sophisticated he always insisted on a reduction. Women, who then as now did most of the buying, prided themselves on their ability to judge the quality of goods and to win out in arguments with clerks. Timid women seldom shopped alone but would work in pairs to bring greater pressure to bear on the shopkeeper. These shopping encounters often left the customer with a feeling that the merchant had gotten the better of the bargain and there was a feeling of hostility between customer and shopkeeper difficult to understand today.

This method of selling was extremely expensive. Old

account books show that before the days of fixed prices and retail advertising the storekeeper had to employ two or three times as many clerks as needed today to sell the same quantity of goods. This meant of course that he had to add a much higher percentage of profit to take care of the overhead of a big force of salesmen. Even the lowest possible price secured after lengthy arguments, usually represented a margin of profit the merchant of today would not think of asking. The cost of selling was handed on to the buyer as it must always be in any system of merchandising.

The first step on the road to honest goods at honest prices came with the adoption of the one price policy. A. T. Stewart who opened a small shop in New York with a three thousand dollar stock of linen and laces was too busy to waste time arguing with customers and too thrifty to employ unnecessary clerks. Perhaps he realized that if his clerks did not have to be clever bargainers he would not have to employ such expensive talent. Whatever the reason may have been, he announced that the prices of all goods in his shop were marked in plain figures and nothing would be sold at a lower price. This unusual trade announcement was looked on by sophisticated New Yorkers as a clever advertising dodge—something that would get the little shop talked about and arouse the curiosity of customers. It did both. But when shoppers started their usual tactics of beating down the price they were very much surprised to find that the announcement meant just what it said. Nothing like this had ever happened before. Women shoppers were insulted at Stewart's unflinching attitude and threatened to boycott the place. Some did stay away but business grew so fast that in less than a year the shop was too small and Stewart moved into larger quarters.

Rival storekeepers looked enviously at Stewart's success

and many announced a similar policy. [With some the old system had been followed too long to be easily discarded. Rather than allow an old customer to escape, price concessions would be made. Stewart had the advantage over his competitors because his was a new shop with no old customers, no bad merchandising habits to break. Perhaps that is the reason he outdistanced them all in the competition for the rapidly growing retail trade of New York City. Having established a reputation for fixed prices, he frequently advertised bargain sales in different departments, which were very successful. People knew that the price reductions he advertised were genuine. Slowly the public learned that the merchant who has more than one price is not honest. The single fixed price policy was generally adopted before the Civil War. In the meantime, Stewart's success had been so great that his original three thousand dollars had grown to a large fortune. He invested almost three million dollars in a mammoth building and had the largest store in the world.

While full credit is due to Stewart for this great early reform in retail selling, it was a reform that no one could have inaugurated at a much earlier date. Honest prices had to await the production of honest goods of standard uniform quality, and this had to wait the replacement of handicrafts by machine production. When all articles were made by hand, no two were ever exactly alike and there was always a fair amount of defective merchandise that had to be disposed of at whatever price the merchant could get. As fixed prices became general, the whole method of selling in retail stores was changed. Clerks could no longer argue about price; the only thing they could talk about was quality. Both merchant and customer became increasingly conscious of quality, and demanded more rigid standards of manufacture. Stewart's price policy created a new relationship of friendship and confidence between customer and merchant, and slowly merchants began to accept a new responsibility, that of protecting the interests of their customers both as to quality and price.

Charles Tiffany was born in 1812 and by the time he was twenty-five years old a good many New Yorkers were prosperous enough to buy in considerable quantities merchandise that was not actually essential. The carriage trade was beginning to assume some importance as a symbol of a clientele of customers with taste and discrimination. Not too long after that every picture of a New York store building showed a waiting carriage and coachman at the curb, clearly indicating that it was patronized by the best people. Tiffany's small "stationery and fancy goods shop" which catered to this new trade was really the first gift shop in the United States. The stock, all of which was imported, consisted of Japanese fans, Chinese porcelains, Malacca canes, and other gadgets of the day that people might buy but could certainly do without. The shop was opened in September and sales were discouragingly small until the day before Christmas when they rocketed to $236. At that time the New Year was a more important holiday than Christmas and the sales on the last day of December amounted to $675.

With a steady and growing volume of business in prospect, Tiffany inaugurated a few years later a new method of securing the kind of merchandise wanted by the people who came to his store regularly and in increasing numbers. Like some other merchants, he was beginning to think of them as clients rather than as customers. He was the first American merchant to take the initiative in the important function of supplying himself with goods. American manufacturers had

connections with jobbers or commission agents to whom
they consigned the product of their factories. Salesmen of
these concerns called on merchants, displayed their line and
made sales. Importers brought over cargo on speculation and
sold it in the same way. Not only was it an expensive method
of distributing goods but it left a gap between consumer and
producer which made it difficult for the latter to keep in
close touch with what is now known as "consumer demand,"
a phrase unknown in 1841.

Tiffany's customers wanted little luxury articles out of the
ordinary run of merchandise. In order to supply this demand
he inaugurated the system of sending buyers to Europe where
they picked up such novelties as cheap German jewelry—
stuff that Tiffany of a hundred years later would scorn to put
in a basement sale—but it pleased and satisfied New Yorkers
of that day. This was not all the Tiffany buyers brought back.
They found that Europe was in chaos and that diamonds
could be bought at very cheap prices. With an article like a
diamond it was more than ever necessary for the merchant,
the honest merchant, to do a little more than just refrain
from questionable selling methods. Most of the people who
bought diamonds had never owned one before, had no way
of knowing the genuine from the many imitations which
were on the market. Diamonds were novelties to Tiffany
himself, for when he started his shop his whole capital
represented little more than the price of a good solitaire.
But he and other Tiffany men learned the diamond business
so that they could see that their clients got genuine gems at
reasonable prices. At about the same time John Wanamaker
in Philadelphia was studying the ready-made clothing business with similar objects in view.

The idea that a merchant should travel far from home

Our grandmothers wore a lot of clothes

A SOAP-CERTIFICATE.

I used your soap two years ago and have not used any other since.

THE BEST SOAP MADE IS

JAS. S. KIRK & CO'S WHITE RUSSIAN.

A famous advertisement for a famous soap

A fashionably dressed young gentleman mows an ornate lawn

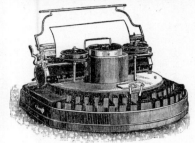
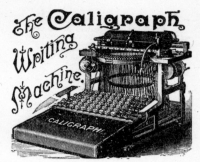
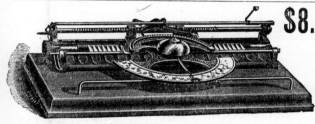
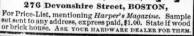

No house was complete without a porch

Douglas sold shoes for gentlemen for $3

The Sargent Manufacturing Co.'s
SPECIALTIES.
THINGS PRACTICAL.

FIG. 1.

FIG. 2.

FIG. 3.

FIG. 5.

FIG. 4.

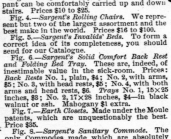

FIG. 6.

FIG. 9.

Figs. 1 and 2.—*Sargent's Monarch Reclining Chair.* As an ordinary easy-chair or for invalids' use it is the finest Reclining Chair in the world. Over 300 positions. Prices $50 to $125. We have also a great variety of other styles of Reclining Chairs from $10 up.

Fig. 3.—*Sargent's Carrying Chairs.* The occupant can be comfortably carried up and down stairs. Prices $10 to $25.

Fig. 4.—*Sargent's Rolling Chairs.* We represent but two of the largest assortment and the best make in the world. Prices $16 to $100.

Fig. 5.—*Sargent's Invalids' Beds.* To form a correct idea of its completeness, you should send for our Catalogue.

Fig. 6.—*Sargent's Solid Comfort Back Rest and Folding Bed Tray.* These are, indeed, of inestimable value in the sick-room. Prices: *Back Rests* No. 1, plain, $4; No. 2, with arms, $5; No. 3, with head rests, $5; No. 4, with both arms and head rests, $6. *Trays* No. 1, 15×25 inches, $3; No. 2, 17×28 inches, $4—in black walnut or ash. Mahogany $1 extra.

Fig. 7.—*Earth Closets.* Made under the Moule patents, which are unquestionably the best. Price $35.

Fig. 8.—*Sargent's Sanitary Commode.* The only Commodes made which are absolutely odorless. We make all kinds as well. Prices $5 to $25.

Fig. 9.—*Sargent's Table Universelle.*—A marvel of utility and beauty for the library or sick-room.

Fig. 10.—*A Place for the Dictionary.* Adjustable as well to any book, any height or any angle. Price $5.

Fig. 11.—*Dictionary Holder with Reference-Book Revolving Case.* One of the most useful and practical things for anybody's use. Price $9.

Fig. 13.—*The Perfection Adjustable Reading and Writing Desk.*—Can be attached to any chair. The only *real good* one in the market. Price $3.50 to $5.

Fig. 14.—*The Cabinet Revolving Book-case.* Three sizes. Prices $16, $19, and $22.

NOTE.—These cuts can give but a faint idea of our extensive stock. We have the most complete stock of goods in the world for the comfort and luxury of both the sick and the well. Our Catalogue of 80 pages illustrates and explains everything in detail, with prices, etc. Sent free by addressing

THE SARGENT MANUFACTURING CO.,
814 and 816 Broadway, New York.

FIG. 10.

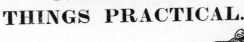

FIG. 11.

FIG. 12.

THE ORIGINAL

UTILITY

Adjustable-Folding Table.

PRICE $6 UP.

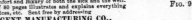

FIG. 13.

FIG. 14.

The latest in household comforts and conveniences
when Hayes was president

and go to considerable expense in order to buy goods for his customers was as new as the idea that goods should be sold at fixed prices; but it was sound and was soon adopted by other merchants. We were passing out of the homespun era and customers were becoming more exacting not only in the matter of quality but in their demands on the manufacturer, telling him what they wanted to buy rather than taking what he had to sell. The new purchasing system enabled the merchant to stock goods for which there was a greater demand and hence make a quicker turnover, with a consequent saving in selling costs. We were on our way toward that merchandising marvel—the modern department store.

Slowly but steadily the American retail merchant adopted what might be called a kind of protective attitude toward his customers. By reason of his experience and, in some cases, technical knowledge, he was a better judge of quality than the customer could be and he knew where and how to secure merchandise at the cheapest prices. John Wanamaker assumed this responsibility to the extent that he became a manufacturer of men's clothing in order to make sure that the suits he sold did not fall below the standard of quality he had set for his Philadelphia store. For some time this responsibility for quality rested entirely with the merchant, who had to inspect carefully every article brought into his shop. This was progress from the time when the responsibility had to be borne by the individual customer. The next step came when the manufacturers began branding their products with their own trade names and advertising them thus, finally placing responsibility for standard quality where it rightly belonged— on the shoulders of the man who made the goods. No one need be a merchandising expert or more than an amateur economist to see how each step in this program not only gave the public better merchandise but lowered the cost by ironing out the bottlenecks in distribution.

Reforms in manufacturing and merchandising did not come all at once but were spread over the better part of a century, affecting different lines at different times. As early as 1810 Eli Terry was making clocks of established reputation and about the same time a seedsman at Hartford was selling vegetable seeds in packages bearing his name. The Collins axes came into the field soon after, and there followed the long struggle to reform the business of making men's ready-made clothing. There were innumerable defects in textiles, some because of lack of technical skills, others the result of deliberate chicanery. Printed calicoes faded because we were inexpert in the use of dyes, but that was not the reason that flannels when taken home did not represent the yardage bought at the store. It was the custom to attach them to the bolt and to stretch them to their fullest capacity.

Food products were among the last to come under the influence of the merchandise reformers, that is, the merchants who were protecting the interests of their customers. There is today, and always will be, a certain amount of food adulteration, but nothing so crude as the common practices of a hundred years ago on both sides of the Atlantic. Owing to the development of the cotton trade, there was a close business association between New York and Liverpool, and the papers of the two cities for years carried on good-natured controversies as to which city suffered the most at the hands of the wholesale grocers. In New York it was common practice to mix pounded rice with granulated sugar. No prudent housewife would buy anything but green coffee berries which were roasted and ground in her own kitchen. Ready ground coffee was not on sale. Roasted coffee was sold, but some slicker had found a method of molding a chicory composition into the form of a coffee berry. Cocoa was adulterated with brown clay in which mutton fat had been mixed to give it the correct oily consistency. Pepper was mixed with any kind of dust of the appropriate color just as dried leaves of trees and shrubs were mixed with tea. These adulterations continued until foods were packaged and sold by an advertised brand name—a development that came about within the memory of many living men.

Cities grew in size but the growth of the department stores had to wait the development of horsecars and elevators. Even in the early days when people did a lot more walking than they do now, shoppers would not climb flights of stairs to the upper floors, so that stores could only grow laterally. John Wanamaker's "Grand Depot" which amazed visitors at the Centennial Exposition in Philadelphia in 1876 was a large barn-like structure of only one floor which had been built for use as a tabernacle for a Moody and Sankey revival.

The small one-man neighborhood shop, colorful but inefficient, persisted until electricity brought cheap and convenient travel to shopping centers, elevators made it unnecessary to climb the stairs, and the incandescent light made it possible to shop on dark days. The department store offered a greater variety of goods and at cheaper prices. Similar establishments in England appropriately refer to themselves as "universal providers."

The last of the small shops to fall into line with modern merchandising methods were the drugstores. In 1883 there were 600 of them in New York and a prominent member of the trade estimated that they averaged a gross turnover of about twenty-five dollars a day. According to the same authority, half of this consisted of the highly ethical business of filling prescriptions, the other half of the sale of Warner's Safe Cure for Consumption, Lydia E. Pinkham's Vegetable Compound, Snake Root, and other proprietary remedies of doubtful value, on which the stores made a large profit. There was also a small business in the sale of tooth brushes and dentifrices. The typical business was run by the pharmacist and a boy.

The problem which was agitating the druggists at that time and continued to agitate them for several years was whether or not they were tradesmen. This was not snobbery but reflected the druggist's concern over his anomalous position. Behind the prescription counter he was a professional man doing a job of work that only a professional man could do. At the same time, in the patent medicine department he was selling nostrums which offered direct and irritating competition to the doctor whose prescriptions he filled. No wonder druggists were in a quandary as to just what their status was.

About this time the question was solved for them by the flood of new articles which were coming into the market—things such as fountain pens, and attractively packaged cosmetics. These and other articles took up little room and could be displayed to advantage in the small drugstores, while they were lost in the larger shops. Within a decade the rows of gilt labeled bottles which had dominated the main room of every drugstore were moved back behind a partition, and the shelves were filled with a great variety of small merchandise. Druggists put in larger plate glass windows and began signing leases for shops on corners. They were definitely tradesmen and they were soon to become restaurant keepers.

Great fortunes were made by many of these merchants who concerned themselves solely with the retail trade. The result was that a new class of people was attracted to this branch of merchandising. The retail business had formerly been confined to small shops conducted by men whose ambition was to make enough money to get into the wholesale trade, for it was here, according to popular belief, that big money could be made. Stewart, Wanamaker, Marshall Field, and a host of others who sprang up and flourished all over the country demonstrated that the retail merchant had a genuine and useful function to perform—that fortunes awaited the merchant who served his customers by providing them with honest goods at honest prices. In building up a profitable trade for himself by catering to the needs of his fellow man, the retail merchant and the manufacturer were performing a social service of which they were probably entirely unconscious. And by becoming rich through honest methods they justified personal wealth as it had never been justified before. There was a very narrow limit to the amount of money the petty retail shopkeeper might make in a long and busy lifetime. The proprietors of these great emporiums with their huge turnover might with a small margin of profit make as much in a single day.

It is curious that these American merchants who introduced such a high standard of business ethics into the retail business were contemporaries of the greatest gang of commercial crooks the country has ever known. Wall Street, crooked officials, and professional thieves were in close collaboration. Railway officials not only manipulated their own stock but sold forged issues. During this period when business chicanery in high places was the rule rather than the exception, the retail trade established a standard of ethics previously unknown in the world's history.

Chapter XIV

COMMERCE WITHOUT CURRENCY

THE business life of the United States started with an almost complete absence of the one thing presumably essential to all commercial transactions, and that was money. This did not imply any transition from conditions during colonial days, for the limited business of the colonies was carried on with an even more limited supply of any kind of currency. In fact, one of the first things the early settlers did was to wreck a system of currency that was quite adequate to the needs of the Indians, and many years elapsed before anything was provided to take its place. Wampum which circulated among both the Indians and whites was nothing more than periwinkle shells in which a hole had been drilled, strung together with a thong and sometimes woven into a belt. It wasn't of any more utility in itself than is a wallet full of bank notes, but it did represent wealth as produced by labor—a great deal of labor. The holes were drilled with a pointed flint and the work was so tedious that there was no danger of inflation through the production of too much wampum.

By a very simple logical process the Indians justified their acceptance of this as currency. They thought that if one of their fellows was willing to spend days drilling holes in shells and stringing them on thongs, there was no reason why he should not be rewarded for his labor by having the strings accepted in payment for a blanket or a handful of corn or anything else that was on the market. Even such a valuable article as a canoe might be bought with wampum.

The system worked very well until the arrival of the white man. According to New England accounts, the collapse of this simple system was due to the manipulation of the avaricious and unscrupulous Dutch settlers in New Amsterdam. These early financiers found plenty of suitable sea shells on the shores of Long Island Sound and by using steel drills pierced a hundred shells in the time it would take an Indian with his flint drill to pierce a half dozen. The Dutch soon had great stores of mass production wampum which gave them a decided advantage in trading with the Indians. The New Englanders, with their deep religious convictions, were greatly shocked by this chicanery and advised the Indians not to accept the steel-drilled wampum, which they called "devil's currency."

However, the Dutch were very successful in using their currency to purchase beaver pelts from the Indians; in order to avoid being crowded out of the trade, the New Englanders forgot their conscientious scruples and met unfair competition by unfair methods. They set up their own wampum factories and runaway inflation was the inevitable result. Wampum constantly decreased in value, though for a long time it was possible to unload it on the Indians at an advantageous exchange rate. Finally even the Indians would not accept it, and so it was necessary to trade them glass beads, rum, and gunpowder. New Englanders never ceased blaming the Dutch for initiating these sinful practices.

Nothing was provided to take the place of wampum. The pounds, shillings, and pence of England were used in reckoning accounts but very few of the actual coins were in circulation. We shipped beaver pelts, lumber, tobacco, potash, and dried fruit to England, but we got cloth, pewterware, mousetraps, and other manufactured goods in return. If the value of the goods shipped by the colonial exporter exceeded the value of the goods he received the difference was more than likely to be placed to the credit of his account on the books of the London merchant. All export and import trade was carried on an open account and it was not often that the books were balanced by a cash settlement. If the colonial exporter had a credit to his account, he ordered more goods; if a debit, he shipped more produce. Some silver coins did come in from trading with Barbados and the West Indian ports, and a little gold. But there was a constant diminution of gold and silver currency brought into the colonies. The big Spanish silver dollars were melted down or just beaten into platters, teapots, spoons, and dram cups. They were worth just as much in that form as in coins and were not so easily stolen or lost. Actually very few perfect coins ever reached the colonists, as it was the custom to "sweat" them, thus reducing the silver content or to nick out small pieces of silver. Gold coins were treated in the same way and were often converted into the solid gold beads which every fashionable woman wore.

There were no banks in colonial days and the only people who could compute the value of the various foreign coins were the gold- and silversmiths who knew how to test the fineness of the coins and had delicate scales with which to weigh them. The result was that the silversmith was a rather important man in his community and often acted as town treasurer. If anyone could judge the credit rating of the local people, he could, because he knew who had valuable silver plate stored away and its approximate value.

In 1783 when Paul Revere received a cargo of London merchandise with which to start his Boston shop, he paid for it with the miscellaneous assortment of precious metal that passed as currency almost all over the world. Part of the payment was made in Spanish silver dollars. These were well minted coins which the Spanish were able to produce in great quantities because of the silver which Pizarro, Cortez, and other conquistadores had pilfered from Mexico, Peru, and other conquered territories. According to the modern interpretation of the term, the Spanish dollar was not a coin. It was just a weight of silver bearing the trade-mark of the Spanish government. A pound of these minted dollars was worth approximately as much as a pound of silver ingots which Revere melted down and cast from the sweepings in his shop.

While coins were scarce in the ports, they were even rarer in the interior, and the colonists out of necessity used other media of exchange, placing their trust in some commodity which was widely produced and readily marketable. In Virginia quite naturally the commodity was tobacco. A great many old inventories which were compiled in settling estates fixed the value of pieces of furniture and even of real property in number of pounds of tobacco. In New York and some parts of New England debts could be paid in beaver pelts and at a later date taxes in Missouri could be paid in coonskins. A great deal of trading was also done with honey, wild turkeys, and venison. In 1848 merchants in San Francisco advertised:

"Lowest prices in either cash or hides."

A great many different commodities were used in place of money in different colonies and states at different times, including tar, potash, hemp, and flax. The use of commodities in place of currency was greatly simplified by the fixing of an arbitrary exchange value which had no legal status but was generally accepted. Thus at one time a bushel of corn or ten pounds of butter was presumed to be equivalent in value to a pound of handmade nails. These exchange values were not always legalized but were customarily accepted. A Virginia statute of 1682 made flax, hemp, tar, lumber, and washed wool legal tender for the payment of debts. The following year Pennsylvania enacted similar legislation regarding flax and hemp, the former at eight pence, the latter at four pence per pound. In 1674 Rhode Island fixed the price of wool at twelve pence a pound. At various times both Massachusetts and New Hampshire made leather, turpentine, hemp, and tar legal tender for the payment of taxes. With actual payment in coin entering into few transactions, few accounts of any sort were ever settled. With the constant trading or swapping that went on in each community, it was possible for any one member of the community to be in debt to or to have money coming from almost all of his neighbors. Business could only be conducted by the use of long and liberal credit terms. The "credit dollar" enabled Americans to transact a very large amount of business during a period when a very small amount of money of any kind was in circulation.

The great scarcity of money was reflected in the arrangement usually made for the support of a minister. He was provided with a house suitable for a dwelling, the revenue from ten to twenty acres of pasture land, all the wood he needed, and a salary which was sometimes as small as a hundred dollars a year. If he served the dominant Congregational sect the salary would be a part of the village or township budget and would be met by tax funds. There was in every community a committee to manage the minister's supply of wood, that is, to see that it was cut and stored in the woodshed before winter set in.

Peace with England had scarcely been concluded when steps were taken to set up a mint and establish a national coinage. Some rough silver dollars had been coined during the Revolution. When no more silver was available, some dollars were made of pewter but they were not popular, even among the most patriotic. A report which was presented to Congress recommended the adoption of a decimal system— a newfangled French idea that Jefferson had seen in operation in Paris. A paragraph of the report read:

"Although it is not absolutely necessary, yet it is very desirable, that money should be increased in a decimal ratio; because by that means all calculations of interest, exchange, insurance and the like, are rendered much more simple and accurate, and of course more within the powers of the great mass of the people."

There was opposition to this radical move but Jefferson held out and argued for it. After recounting in detail the difficulty encountered in multiplying a sum of English money he said:

"The bulk of mankind are school boys throughout life. Certainly in all cases, where we are free to choose between easy and difficult modes of operation, it is most rational to choose the easy. The financier, therefore, well proposes that our coins should be in decimal proportions to each other."

The decimal system was adopted, but in spite of its convenience people continued to think of money in terms of pounds, shillings, and pence, and old business firms did not convert their books into the new currency. As a matter of fact, when Jefferson was president he kept his personal accounts in English currency.

The new mint did not actually get into operation until more than ten years after independence was established and in its first year of actual operation in 1795 it produced less than two million individual coins of gold, silver, and copper, worth a total value of $192,129.40. With a population of about five million that was a little less than four cents per capita! The total coinage of the country would buy a five cent candy bar for only four-fifths of the people! It was with this pitifully small amount of cash in circulation that our pioneer businessmen began to make their plans for the future.

It was not until the present century that the mints began turning out great quantity and that the copper had any purchasing value reckoned by merchants and manufacturers. Forty years ago banks in Texas and other parts of the Southwest and the West completely ignored the one cent coin. The nickel was the smallest coin in their vaults.

The first mint was in Philadelphia, but in 1835 three branch mints were established. One of these was at New Orleans where considerable quantities of foreign coins were collected. The other two were located in what were then the two most important gold-producing centers in the United States, Charlotte in North Carolina and Dahlonega in Georgia. These early mints are remembered only by coin collectors but it was in them that our first gold coins were produced. A visitor to Dahlonega in Civil War days refers to the place as "riddled with mines."

The new mints were modeled after European models and the old Philadelphia mint was improved. The production of coins was speeded up, but the stock in circulation accumulated very slowly. On January 1, 1844, the total value of American coins that had been minted amounted to just a little more than one hundred million dollars. If this amount had been equally divided it would have meant that every man, woman, and child in our population of seventeen million would have had in his or her possession the approximate sum of $6.02. This would have consisted of $2.30 in gold, $3.66 in silver, and six of the copper one cent pieces which were almost as large as the present half dollar. Obviously the time was not ripe for a penny in the slot machine!

This was sixty years after the peace treaty with England. We had made a good deal of progress in developing small factories and establishing efficient distribution of goods. This had been possible only because the old barter system of colonial days continued. Farmers traded their produce to the country stores and received credit for it against their purchases. The storekeeper shipped the produce to the city market where he also was credited on the books of the wholesale concern. The country stores issued "due bills," another substitute for coins which found wide circulation.

There was not enough money in circulation to meet the payroll demands of the few small factories and as a result an adaptation of the old apprentice system was carried over into the developing factory system. The Seth Thomas clock factory was, for the period, a large employer of labor, for it started with twenty hands in addition to teamsters who hauled the completed clocks to Boston. The number of people on the payroll of this successful enterprise constantly grew, but there was no weekly or even monthly pay day. Workmen lived in houses owned by the company, bought provisions, clothing, and other necessities at the company store. Earnings were credited and purchases debited and the books were balanced once a year when the workman was paid the balance due him. He could draw money before the annual settlement day only "in case of an emergency," which implied either illness or death.

That was the typical method of paying wages during the

first quarter of last century. A history of Pittsfield, Massachusetts, tells of the proprietor of a forge who would put an iron bar over his shoulder and carry it to a shop, where he would trade it for provisions for his workmen, which he carried back in the same way. That was the only way of doing business. There is no reason to believe that the early iron founders or clockmakers profiteered by charging their workmen an excessive price for the provisions they supplied, but there was plenty of chicanery of this sort in the sweat-shop manufacture of ready-made clothing. The company store was something of a necessity in the small towns where most of the New England factories were started, but not in Boston, New York, and Philadelphia, which were centers of the clothing industry. Yet the manufacturers compelled their employees to accept orders on coal companies and grocery stores in which they were interested.

The custom of trading in commodities or saleable merchandise continued long after any necessity for it existed. Connecticut clockmakers, for example, had traded their clocks for provisions and raw material in the shape of metal scrap and had paid iron furnace proprietors in clocks for the weights that they bought. They did not pay cash for anything if it was at all possible to trade clocks instead. Thus it was quite natural that when one clockmaker, Eli Terry, sold a house to another clockmaker, Chauncey Jerome, he should be paid for it in clocks, receiving exactly 214. Later Terry bought a house for himself for which he paid three hundred clocks.

Chapter XV

THE ERA OF THE KEROSENE LAMP

WHETHER or not early going to bed and early rising would, as Franklin said, make one wealthy as well as healthy and wise, may be debatable. But there can be no doubt but that in his day and for many years after that, getting to bed early was the thrifty thing to do. It cost a lot in money and time to provide any illumination good enough to make sitting up at night enjoyable. The homemade tallow dip candle was about the cheapest illuminant available. If made at home from tallow produced on the farm they didn't cost much of anything but labor. But their production was tedious—one of the most tedious of the many farm tasks. The wick was dipped into melted tallow, withdrawn and allowed to cool, then dipped in again. With each dipping a little more tallow adhered to the wick until finally there was a candle. The feeble light which it gave for an hour or so, had been paid for by tedious dipping in a kettle of hot tallow. Molded candles could be made with much less labor and were much more attractive in appearance. But candle molds were expensive and not every family could afford one. The lady who was able to display neatly molded candles in her home belonged to a social class quite distinct from those who could afford nothing better than the humble tallow dip.

Long before night clubs were dreamed of, sitting up nights was expensive—just sitting up—with no cover charge. Very few did and soon after sundown the only lights visible in a town would be shining through the windows of taverns where men drank rum and talked politics in a subdued light much like that to be found in some modern cocktail lounges. Quite naturally displays of fireworks were more popular then than now.

Sperm candles which were made in factories are mentioned frequently in accounts of colonial life, but they were too expensive to have been generally used except in lighting churches and in the homes of the rich. Much more common on the farms were rush lights, prepared at home by soaking dried reeds in lard or any other kind of household grease. The pith of the reed, being impregnated with fats, would give off a fairly consistent flame. The light was poor, the rush soon burned out and while it was burning it smoked up the room. One thing that could be said for it was that it was a more satisfactory reading light than that supplied by the burning logs in the fireplaces. This was a common method of illuminating humble homes in America for more than two hundred years.

In the early days of the republic there was no very great demand for better or cheaper lights except from the limited number of intelligentsia who wanted to sit up nights reading books or discussing weighty matters with their colleagues. Artificial illumination played no part in industry. Factories ran only in daylight hours, the usual working day being from sunrise to sunset. In the small factories the fourteen-hour working day of summer was shortened to ten in winter. These were also the hours when shops were open.

This satisfaction with inadequate lighting did not long continue. As towns grew into cities, some form of street lighting became necessary and this problem was solved much earlier than the problem of illumination for homes. Gas lighting had been tried out in London and in 1816 the proprietor of a Baltimore museum lighted his establishment with this new illuminant. Never before had Americans seen a room so brilliantly illuminated at night, and the museum was talked about all over the country. Without delay the Baltimore authorities arranged for street lighting by gas and other cities followed suit, but very slowly. Iron pipes were expensive, freight rates and coal were high. The first gas pipes laid in London consisted of musket barrels. Ignorance and superstition played their parts in delaying progress. People objected to having pipes containing this inflammable substance laid under or near their houses. However, gas plants were erected for street lighting; but gas was not generally used for lighting homes until after the Civil War. Improved methods of making iron pipe had by that time lowered the cost of laying mains, and lower freight rates had brought down the price of coal; but gas lighting was still very expensive. Rates charged for gas were five to ten times those now charged.

Most of the people lived on farms or in small towns, and they continued to use candles, rushes, and pine splinters. The smelly lamps in which a lighted wick burned melted lard had been developed; but when whale oil became available these lamps were discarded for those using the new oil, and a new odor was added to the mixed collection which permeated American homes. The oil of the sperm whale provided a better light than most Americans had ever seen. John Adams had said of sperm oil: "It gives the clearest and most beautiful flame of any substance known to nature." But sperm oil came only from the head of one kind of a whale, and it was always expensive, selling for as much as three dollars a gallon. It is not surprising that whale oil lamps should have been equipped with such tiny wicks. Illumination by lard oil cost less. In spite of the poor light and the difficulty about keeping the lard melted, some of these lamps were in use until just before the Civil War.

As education advanced and Americans became a nation of newspaper readers, the daylight hours became too short for an increasing number of people. Many experimenters tried to find an illuminant which would be cheaper than sperm oil. Attempts to produce an oil from coal were finally successful and soon oil was actually produced in this way, though little of it was sold, for it was smoky and generally unsatisfactory. In 1850 a plant was established in Brooklyn for the manufacture of an illuminating oil which was produced by distilling wood and resin together in a jet of high steam pressure. Special lamps were made for the use of this oil, but like the oil made from coal the product was not entirely satisfactory. The lamps smoked and gave off a foul odor. Other lamps were made for burning raw turpentine, but these were too inflammable for general use.

For several decades inventors on both sides of the Atlantic were busy trying to improve methods of producing an illuminating oil out of coal or wood or to devise a lamp in which turpentine could be burned without serious danger of setting the house on fire. No one was especially interested in lubricants. Steam engines were lubricated by mutton tallow, the heavy moving parts of rolling mills by pork fat. Sometimes a side of pork would be strapped to the bearings of a machine. Lard was a general lubricant for all light machinery, except in the cotton mills where olive oil was preferred, as it could be washed out of the fabric without leaving a stain. These, with castor oil and whale oil, supplied every conceivable need of industry. The great need was for a good cheap illuminating oil for the man who could not afford gas lights or who lived in small towns where they were not available.

With the insistent and growing demand for a cheap illuminating oil, it is surprising that the discovery of the value of the oil seeping out of the ground and fouling the creeks of Pennsylvania was so long delayed. For more than a hundred years travelers had noted the presence of oil here, and for more than fifty years farmers living in the neighborhood had been complaining about the presence of the slime that fouled the creeks so that the stock would not drink the water. The processes of distillation had been pretty well known since the first part of the century—had been used to refine turpentine and to produce an illuminating oil from coal.

Well drillers knew that petroleum was to be found in quantities beneath the surface of the earth, because many of them had encountered it when drilling for brine from which to make salt. Chemists knew that a substance like this could be distilled to produce illuminating oil, because that had been done successfully with less promising substances such as coal, resin, and wood. In fact, petroleum had been distilled into kerosene by a Pittsburgh druggist in 1840, or soon thereafter.

Medical quacks who traveled about the country selling nostrums with their Indian medicine shows sold a lot of this oil, which they claimed would cure "cholera morbus, laryngitis, rheumatism and consumption. Good for man or beast, for lungs, liver or lights." They obtained the oil by soaking blankets in the streams where seepages occurred and then wringing out the blankets.

The oil had been used by the Seneca Indians of Pennsylvania for ceremonial and medical purposes as well as for mixing their war paints. Samuel M. Kier, a Pittsburgh druggist, sold the patent medicines of the day, and it occurred to him that he might go into the patent medicine business with great profit to himself by bottling and selling this Indian remedy. His advertising claims were no more extravagant than those made for all patent medicines. A descriptive circular which was wrapped around each bottle read:

KIER'S

Petroleum or rock oil, celebrated for its wonderful curative powers. A natural remedy. Procured from well in Allegheny Co., Pa., four hundred feet below the earth's surface. Put up and sold by Samuel M. Kier, 363 Liberty Street, Pittsburgh, Pa.

PRICE 50 CENTS

In order to lend an air of authenticity to the statement about the four hundred foot well, the circular was embellished with a picture of a well derrick like that used in drilling brine wells. The statement about the four hundred foot well was doubtless a harmless myth, but Kier must have had a generous and reliable source of supply, for it is said that he disposed of three barrels of the oil daily. Then faith in the oil as a medicine began to wane and sales fell off. Kier now tried the experiment of distilling the oil to produce a refined product suitable for burning in lamps. His experiments were successful; but there the matter rested. Perhaps he did not realize that the distilling process he had carried out on a restricted laboratory scale could be duplicated in giant plants, which could thus supply oil for millions of lamps. He may have been disappointed at slow sales or small profits. A man who had been selling crude petroleum at fifty cents for a ten ounce bottle might well have had his head turned by the fetish of quick and easy profits. He was not the first American druggist to let a fortune slip from his grasp. Only a few years before this a New England druggist had invented a friction match, but as he was disappointed in the sales he sold the formula to others who developed the product and made millions out of it. The New England druggist got ten dollars. Kier got nothing. He had constructed the first kerosene refinery, a tiny affair consisting of a small iron pot with a crude worm, not unlike a still used by moonshiners.

More than ten years after his experiments, others who had ample capital and more technical knowledge began the successful exploitation of petroleum and changed the course of events that make history. A bottle of petroleum on the desk of a Dartmouth College professor attracted the attention of George Bissell, a business man with more experience and vision than Kier. He sent a sample of the oil to a professor of chemistry at Yale, who analyzed it and made a favorable report. Bissell decided to go into the oil business. His initial investment was not a very large one—only five thousand dollars for the purchase and lease of land in the area where the oil seepages occurred. It was the plan of Bissell, and of the college professor experts who advised him, to dig pits in the ground where it was presumed that the oil would collect in increasing quantities just like water would collect in pits dug in swampy ground. The pits were dug but brought no increase in the flow, and Bissell appears to have done nothing more for a year or so.

In 1856, three years after he had seen the bottle of petroleum at Dartmouth, Bissell read one of Kier's advertisements, presumably for the first time, and noted the picture of the well drilling rig and the statement about the well four hundred feet under the ground. He knew that petroleum had been encountered by brine well drillers and he decided to try drilling. He formed a new company to finance the project.

It is quite possible that if this first oil well had encountered, as many of them later did encounter, hundreds of feet of barren rock without a trace of oil, the project might have been abandoned and it would have been left for a later generation to supply the world with its first cheap and dependable illuminant. Fortunately the oil-bearing strata was near the surface and in a comparatively short time oil was struck and rose to within a few feet of the well top of what is now known as the Drake well. Pumps which were set to work brought out twenty-five barrels a day—a quantity too large for the refineries to handle. That was as much oil as could be extracted from the blubber of a cow whale. A large herd of fat hogs could not produce that much lard oil. A week's flow would produce more oil than had ever been extracted from the largest bull sperm whale ever harpooned. In a short time other wells were to be producing daily more oil than a whaling fleet could bring back after a year's cruise.

The era of petroleum had begun, its early days marked by the wildest kind of stock speculation in which fortunes were made or lost overnight. "Coal Oil Johnny," a figure who was rich today, broke tomorrow, and rich again next day, became a favorite stage character. In fact, for some time it was so easy to make money in stock-selling schemes that many so-called oil men devoted themselves to that unproductive end of the business. The possession of parcels of land in the neighborhood of Titusville, Pennsylvania, where the first oil well had been drilled, was all that was needed as the basis for stock-selling schemes in companies whose shares were limited only by the capacity of printing presses.

But more farsighted men thought of the millions of farmers and small town people who were living in homes dimly lighted or not lighted at all. The success of the first wells showed that hitherto undreamed of quantities of oil could be brought to the surface by drilling, and the first experiments at refining showed that this oil could be turned into the cheapest and at the same time the best illuminant the world had ever known. One wonders what old John Adams would have said about it.

The constructive oil men slowly dissociated themselves from the oil well speculators and market riggers. They were overwhelmed by the possibilities of the market they saw for this new product, though it is doubtful if any of them foresaw more than one scene of the oil drama that was later to be unfolded. They worked to solve problems of marketing and distribution that had never before been encountered. The construction of adequate refineries was only one of them. As other wells were sunk and the flow of oil constantly increased, problems of storage and transportation arose. There were not enough barrels to store the oil. Michigan, which was later to prosper so greatly because of the oil industry, had a foretaste of this prosperity in the great demand for barrels made from Michigan oak. They were produced by the tens of thousands, filled with crude oil at the wells, and floated downstream like logs.

The demand for good illuminating oil is illustrated by the fact that at the time the Drake well was drilled there were no less than fifty-seven coal oil factories scattered throughout the eastern part of the United States producing illuminating oil by various methods of distilling bituminous coal. As soon as large and dependable quantities of petroleum began to appear in the market, the coal oil manufacturers realized that their product was outmoded, and they hastily adapted their equipment to take care of refining the new product. The manufacture of coal oil, itself an infant industry, came to an end so quickly that it left no traditions behind it and it is a forgotten chapter in the history of American industries.

The plants which were now converted into petroleum refineries were all small and, according to modern standards, highly inefficient, and the product poor in quality. But it was better and cheaper than any oil that had yet fed the flame of a wick. More and larger refineries were built, the process improved, frequently as the results of accidents. One of the most important of the early discoveries was made because the man in charge of a still "had a fit" when he went home for supper and so did not cut off the flow of oil at the regular time. When he finally recovered and returned to the refinery, he found that he had unwittingly and unconsciously, in the literal sense, discovered a new process for the production of kerosene. The new methods which followed as a result of this discovery increased the yield of what was known as "illuminating oil" by seventy-five per cent.

Kerosene was the most truly democratic product that American industry had offered to the public—an article everyone could use sold at a price everyone could afford to pay. This was true in spite of the fact that the first "illuminating oil" was very dear, sixty cents a gallon in 1860. But that was less than a third of the price of good sperm oil, and it gave six times as much light. Sperm oil had been the illuminant of the aristocrats because of its clear light and absence of odor. But they used the precious liquid sparingly, pouring it in lamps which held only a few ounces, using small round wicks. The new oil was less than half the price of the very troublesome lard oils and provided more than ten times the amount of light. For the first time in the history of man artificial light was not a luxury.

Here was a product which was in almost universal demand, the demand being greatest in the places most remote from the points of production and centers of distribution—in farms and villages. It could not be packaged like hardware or dry goods and shipped in wooden boxes, nor could it be packed in bags like wheat or potatoes. New methods of distribution were necessary. The oak barrels of Michigan were superseded by wooden tanks built on flat cars, to be followed by steel tank cars and pipe lines. The cost of transportation was constantly lowered until from being the most expensive commodity to transport, it became the least expensive.

With increasing production and more efficient methods of refining, the quality of kerosene was constantly improved and the cost reduced. In 1881, twenty years after the first kerosene was exported from New York, the price had dropped from more than sixty cents to less than thirty cents a gallon. In another ten years it was less than ten cents. Oil refineries were able to boast of their product:

"It is carried wherever a wheel can roll or a camel's foot be planted. The caravans of the Desert of Sahara go laden with astral oil while the elephants of India carry standard white. Ships are constantly loading at our wharves for Japan, India, and the most distant isles of the world."

American petroleum was not only feeding the wicks of millions of lamps in all parts of the world, but lubricating oil which was at first an unimportant by-product was liter-

ally greasing the way for better machinery. Before this time
the only lubricants in general use were animal or vegetable
fats and oils. Steam engines, for example, were oiled with
beef tallows. An old teapot full of tallow was kept on the
steam box where the heat maintained the tallow in a fluid
state. About 1870, machines of various kinds, although they
were still faulty, had reached the highest possible development with the old lubricants.

The first crude oil had been refined into petroleum at
Pittsburgh and here, by chance, it was first used as a lubricant. A man who knew nothing about the oil business and
little about machinery secured a few sample bottles of the
crude oil as it came from the well at Titusville, Pa., and
offered it to the manager of a Pittsburgh cotton mill as an
improved sperm oil. After a test the mill manager pro-
nounced it better than the oil he had been using and gave
the oil man a contract to supply the mill with its requirements—two gallons weekly.

It may have been very satisfactory as a lubricant. The
production from some wells is like that, just as the oil from
some—but not many—will burn in lamps without being
refined. But the oil refineries did not depend on these rare
freaks of nature. In the laboratories they soon set up, there
developed a new profession, that of lubrication engineer.
Inventors and manufacturers of machines were no longer
hampered by the bottleneck of lubrication. By different
processes of refining and other operations they produced a
constantly growing variety of oils designed for special purposes. With these aids old machines could be made to run
faster and new machines of greater precision and delicacy
could be constructed. Indeed if this had been the only contribution to humanity made by the oil wells, it would in

itself have been revolutionary in character. We are accustomed to think that the motorcar and the airplane would not be possible without gasoline. It is equally true that they would not be possible but for the lubricants which, like gasoline, were formerly by-products of the kerosene refineries.

Oil men are now able to say of their product: "In the early days oil was used as a lenitive for rheumatism, for easing bruises, and preventing irritation under heavy horse collars; now it hurls great battleships over oceans faster than railway trains formerly ran. It propels dynamos, lights cities, and generates steam to operate factories and mills. There is scarcely a manufacturing plant in the world that does not depend on oil in a greater or lesser degree as its source of either fuel or lubrication.

"Oil is the wizard that sends the airplane into the skies above and the submarine into the depths of the sea; it has made the automobile, the tractor and the motor truck what they are today; it has brought us the paved street, cheap electricity, and multiplied our agricultural possibilities."

Chapter XVI

TWELVE MONTHS OF HARVEST

IN THE early days of America, food was usually cheap when and if it could be found. The colonists and their immediate descendants, farmers of the hillbilly standard of efficiency who preferred the squirrel rifle to the hoe, saw no reason for back-breaking labor with the forests so full of game and the streams so full of fish. They really didn't settle down to farming until game had been pretty well shot out of the settled parts of the country and fish began to be scarce and wary. For a long period before this, a dearth of gunpowder or fishing tackle would have meant a famine more to be feared than any that could be caused by locusts or drought.

People ate what the season afforded and the luck of the hunter or the fisherman provided. If a deer or a turkey were brought down, a family might chew away at venison for weeks or eat wild turkey until they were nauseated. Pepper brought from distant countries was very expensive, but large quantities were used because it helped to conceal the taste of food that had remained in the pot a little too long to be completely wholesome. Fish were plentiful at certain seasons and at certain places. Fish and game provided such a large portion of food supplies that proprietors of some of the early inns employed hunters and fishermen to keep their larders supplied. The menu depended on what these foragers of field and stream were able to bring in. Later some of the big southern plantation-owners detailed slaves as hunters. For the farmer the squirrel rifle was as indispensable as the hoe. Thus we formed food habits which make us the most gluttonous meat-eaters in the world.

These foods cost no more than the labor of bringing them into the kitchen and were dirt cheap when they were procurable. There were times, of course, when the fishing was poor, other times when deer and wild turkeys could not be bought for any price. With many of the early settlers it was the same kind of a "feast or famine" existence the Indians had enjoyed or endured.

No other food supplies were cheap except fresh vegetables, and then only during the brief growing season. At other times they were as unobtainable as wild geese in the winter. Salt, sugar, flour, tea, coffee, cheese, beans, peas—in fact the whole limited line of cereals, seasonings, condiments, and dairy products available about 1800 cost more than now—many times more, if we should take into account the difference in wages. All were of poor quality. Potatoes, though introduced in the old world from America, were practically unknown. Sugar was little more than evaporated molasses in which one could expect to find a generous quantity of insect specimens indigenous to the area where the sugar factories were located, and some very strange and interesting ones from the distant Caribbean. It was sold in rock-like lumps which had to be pulverized before it could be used. Such sugar would not find a market at any price in America today, nor would the pure food laws allow its sale. It cost much more than the best refined sugar now on the market. Sorghum molasses was more commonly used and was known as "long sweetening." Sugar was "short sweetening."

At a time when passenger pigeons could be bought for

one cent each, flour was ten dollars a barrel, a price higher than it has ever been since then except when forced up by war or other artificial conditions. Few could afford to eat wheat bread, and many Americans went to their graves without knowing its taste. It was not until greatly improved harvesting machinery had brought down the price of wheat and better milling methods had reduced the cost of turning wheat into flour that doughnuts and coffee became an American institution. Before that time a doughnut was an expensive form of pastry. Bread made from corn became the staff of life, the South using white corn meal and the North yellow. Even this indigenous product of American soil cost much more than today.

Farm machinery brought down the cost of cereals, made wheat bread available to everyone. Then the tin can, by preserving meats, fish, fruits, and vegetables, bridged the gaps between the seasons and sent food prices down in what has been and continues to be a fairly consistent decline. This economical process enables the packer, whether of fruit, meat, or vegetables, to preserve surplus foods that would otherwise be wasted, and thus spread the blessings of the harvest season throughout the twelve months of the year. Through it the products of each state are available to all the others. California can trade its apricots and asparagus for Maine's corn and lobsters. Thus the tin can in the American kitchen pantry represents a triumph over both time and space. The refrigerator car, the invention of barbed wire, and many other things played later parts in bringing down the cost of food and made greater variation available, but the humble tin can was the pioneer.

Though this method of preserving and distributing food has reached its highest development in America and was given its name by us, its lineage can be traced back to a Napoleonic idea. It was at his suggestion that the French government offered a prize for a practical method of preserving foods—a prize which was won by a Parisian chef in 1810—too late to be of much help in preserving food for Napoleon's armies. The chef sealed the cooked food in glass jars at boiling point heat. The English at once developed this method of preserving food for the growing number of Britons who were living in the distant colonies of the British Empire. The controversy between tin and glass as a container started at that time. The glass bottle or jars the French chef had used were too expensive, so the British turned to the use of cannisters in which tea was packed. Some of this new English product reached America and as the New York bookkeepers wouldn't bother to write out the long name they abbreviated it to *can*, a name which we adopted, though the British prefer the equally short word tin.

As the process antedated by a full twenty years the American invention of a cookstove, the canning of food did not soon become a household industry. In fact, it developed very slowly in the small pioneer packing plants, largely because of the expense of the cans which were cut from the tin plates, shaped, and soldered by hand. A good workman could make ten cans in a day, though improved methods soon increased the production to thirty. Some lobsters, oysters, and salmon were canned as early as 1819, probably for ship stores. Some fruits were also put up in fancy glass bottles for export. A little later corn was canned in Maine. Tomatoes were also canned about the same time. However, the industry made slow progress until 1874, when the retort cooker was invented by a Baltimore canner, making possible the use of heat greater than that of boiling water. Before that time the methods of the commercial canners were as amateurish as those followed by the housewife today. The foods were placed in the cans and the top soldered on leaving a small hole from which the air could escape. Then they were cooked in boiling water and when the process was completed the hole was covered with solder. Canned foods got a bad name they were a long time living down. Defective soldering caused leaks and spoilages. Pinholes in the tin caused trouble. Some foods changed color while in the cover and though this may not have affected the quality, people thought it did. Gases which developed by the decomposition of food actually caused some cans to explode.

With the cooking problem solved, the canners traveled fast and were constantly at the heels of the metal manufacturers demanding cheaper and better cans. As early as 1847 a can-making machine had been invented which did away with much of the old hand labor. It was a marvel of its day, but too slow for the new demands which the canners had found in the American market itself. Gold miners who went to California a few years after this machine was invented longed for their accustomed foods just as the Children of Israel longed for the leeks and onions of the homeland when Moses was leading them through the wilderness. In 1853 a big stock of fresh vegetables was packed in cans for Kane's arctic expedition.

Improved machines later produced cans at the rate of three hundred a minute. A can-closing machine could close and seal 240 cans per minute. The bottom was closed by crimping instead of soldering. Still later a method was devised of closing the cans by crimping, doing away entirely with the use of solder. Production began to be measured in terms of thousands of cases instead of dozens of cans. Machines were devised for automatic packing, for automatic regulation of the degree of heat and the length of time a product should be cooked. Machines labeled the cans and conveyed them to different parts of the plant. Tin sheets of lighter weight were adopted, making the cans easier to open.

Many other machines were devised to reduce the cost of preparing the food for cooking. They include corn huskers and bean snippers. One machine seizes apples floating in water, pares, cores, and quarters them with lightning-like rapidity. The pea viner is perhaps the most marvelous of them all. Vines fresh from the field are fed into the robot which hulls the peas, grades them as to size, and sends them on their way to the cooker. It does the work of two hundred hands. No wonder canned foods are so cheap!

The tin can was only one of many mechanical contrivances which lowered the prices of food in America and brought about a wider distribution throughout the year. The barbed wire fence not only brought a better grade of beef to the market, but also made it possible for western farmers to cultivate their land. There was no timber and no field stone on the plains, and so it was impossible to construct fences like those in the East. Crops could not be cultivated as there was no protection against the roaming herds of cattle. Some tried growing hedges of the Osage orange. This appeared to solve the problem, though the farmers had to wait four years before the fence would be "pig tight, horse high and bull strong." The hedge was cheap for the seed cost only fifty cents a bushel. The demand for seed was great and speculators got hold of the market and raised the price to five dollars a pound. Barbed wire which was invented in 1874 solved the problem. Soon millions of miles of it were made.

Until fences were built, cattle roamed the range breeding in the haphazard fashion of rabbits, and any large scale production of thoroughbred stock was impractical. Range cattle were shipped from Texas, Wyoming, and Montana to the corn-producing sections of the Middle West to be fattened and then shipped to the packing houses. They added enough weight to pay for the corn they consumed but no matter how plump they became, they remained range cattle, tough and stringy. It was taken for granted that a steak would not be edible until the naturally tough fibers of the meat had been broken up by mechanical processes. There was a steak pounder in every household and on a summer morning when the windows were open it was always possible to tell who in the neighborhood was going to have steak for breakfast. The lively tattoo of the steak pounder could be heard blocks away. The hotels and restaurants all had machines resembling small steel rolling mills, some operated by power, in which the steaks were macerated. The heavy demand for devices of this kind is indicated by the large number of patents taken out by inventors of machines in the latter part of the last century. They were commonly known as "steak crushers." The slabs of meat were actually crushed between rollers with sharp points.

Barbed wire made it possible to build fences which cattle could not break through, and so the scientific breeding of cattle brought about the production of steaks which could be eaten without pounding or "crushing." The meat packers, by making use of "everything but the squeal" of a slaughtered animal, operated on a margin of profit that would have brought the old-fashioned butcher to bankruptcy. But the circle of distribution was not complete before the advent of the refrigerator car. The first meat packers made little use of refrigeration. Their principal business was pork packing, the production of hams, bacon, lard, and sausage. They merely did in a large way what had been done in a small way on the farm. Beef for export was cut into chunks and pickled in brine.

A new method for the manufacture of artificial ice was developed, the product became cheaper, and its commercial use was no longer confined to the manufacture of ice cream. Butchers installed ice boxes long before they were common in private homes. The refrigerator car was nothing but a traveling ice box which made it possible to ship meat from the packing house to the most remote village—and has served to perpetuate the meat eating habits we formed when our principal food supply was brought down by a rifle.

With the exception of cereals, wheat, corn, beans, peas, etc., the early American ate only the food produced in his immediate neighborhood. Even cereals were restricted in their distribution because of the high cost of moving them to market. Farmers in western Pennsylvania might have a surplus of corn but could not sell it at a market only a few hundred miles distant because there were no roads, and boats and barges could not be operated because of frozen rivers and canals. Of perishable foods such as fruits and vegetables there was always too much or too little. In most homes there was a dreaded period in the late spring when the supplies in the salt pork barrel began to run low and the vegetable garden had not yet begun to produce.

Food preservation and distribution in America today have been brought to such a high state of perfection that with the exception of a few things such as melons, the seasons have been abolished and food for one community means food for all. In 1800 eight men out of nine were engaged in farming, and produced enough surplus food for the ninth man. Today one out of nine men is a farmer and he produces enough to feed himself and the other eight.

Chapter XVII

BREAD FOR POOR AND RICH

UNTIL just about a hundred years ago the world did not have enough bread to go around and the principal reason for the shortage—in fact the only important reason—was the briefness of the season during which wheat could be harvested. No matter how much of this most important cereal a farmer might plant, his harvest was limited to the amount he could cut and store in the season which lasted from four to eight days. Once the sun turned the heads from green to gold there could be no delay. Grain left in the field after the harvest deadline would shatter and decay.

With the small hand sickle which had been used without improvement for many centuries, two men could harvest a half acre in one day's work, measured from dawn to dark. One man cut the sheaf and laid the several stalks on the ground while the other gathered up the stalks and carried them to the shelter of the barn or beat out the grain with a flail. The harvesting team was usually a man and wife or a father and son. If the yield had been good and the harvest season prolonged by favorable weather they could harvest enough wheat to keep ten people, including themselves, in bread throughout the year. That usually meant that one family of wheatgrowers, with maximum production, could supply itself and one additional family. There were no wheat fields in America as we know them today. Since two men could not harvest more than four acres in eight days, a farmer who planted more than that acreage took a chance that he might have to leave part of it to rot in the fields. Even four acres of wheat was a venture which might prove disastrous in the event of a short season.

The little surplus wheat that found its way to market sold at a high price, and flour was a luxury that only the rich could enjoy. With many farmers wheat was a money crop. They sold their wheat to get cash for taxes and they themselves ate cornbread. Two dollars a bushel was not an unusual price for wheat in colonial days, and flour was correspondingly expensive. George Washington conducted a small mill on his estate at Mt. Vernon and sold flour at thirteen dollars per barrel. If flour sold at that price today the price of bread, crackers, spaghetti, macaroni, and all the other foods that are made from flour would be doubled and there would probably be bread riots. There were riots in New York less than a hundred years ago because most of the people could not afford to buy the flour that was stored in the warehouses.

The old-fashioned wheat cradle which is now outmoded and on its way to the museum was an American invention about the time that Whitney invented the cotton gin. It was first mentioned in 1794. The cradle does not appear to have been the invention of any one man but a gradual development to which many farmer mechanics contributed until it reached its final efficient form. It was possible with the cradle to harvest two acres in a day's work, thus quadrupling the amount of wheat a man could safely plant. Like Whitney's cotton gin, the cradle was a tool any Jack-of-all-trades could make and soon every man who planted wheat owned one. More wheat was grown, but still not enough. Actually the general adoption of the cradle did not lead immediately to a general increase in the acreage planted to wheat. Simple as it was, it was the most complicated tool the farmer had ever been called upon to use, requiring considerable skill in coordination of muscular effort—a swing like that of the golf player. It could not be used by half grown boys and girls who could cut wheat only with a sickle. But the increased acreage did bring down the price of wheat which sold for a dollar and fifty cents a bushel; flour was ten dollars a barrel. The day of the five cent loaf of bread was still as remote as the Lincoln and Douglas debates.

Unlike corn, wheat required no cultivation. It was just planted, grew to maturity without attention, and then was harvested. Corn had to be thinned and plowed in order to produce a crop, but once the corn was ripe it could be left in the field for weeks to be picked like ripe fruit. Since the wheat harvest could not be prolonged, the thoughts of a few farmers turned to machines. If a machine to reap the wheat could be devised, there was no reason why a farmer could not plant a whole forty-acre field in wheat and look forward to harvesting a crop of several hundred bushels.

Quite a number of people other than farmers designed machines to cut wheat and other standing grain. A clergyman drew plans for a six-wheeled chariot equipped with as many giant scissors which would snip off the grain as the vehicle was driven through the field. An actor invented a machine which successfully mowed artificial grain on the stage but wouldn't work in the field. Most of the inventors were baffled by the fact that a machine could not be pulled by horses walking through the ripe grain and they tried to work out some method by which horses could be used to push a machine just as a man pushes a modern lawn mower. The fact that quite a number of patents were issued to these inventors doesn't indicate anything beyond the fact that a great many people were interested in the idea of inventing a mowing machine. For the first forty or fifty years of its existence, the government patent office issued a patent to almost every applicant without bothering to make any investigation.

One of the few practical men who worked on this problem was Robert McCormick, a prosperous Virginia farmer who had made a successful clover huller and other farm equipment for his own convenience. The problem was one in which he was personally interested for Virginia, in the first part of the last century, was the leading wheat-growing state, and he and his neighbors faced a crisis every year when the grain ripened. He worked for years on reaping machines, building them himself in his blacksmith shop on the farm. At each harvest season he would try out his latest improved machine but it never worked in the way he had anticipated. But there was one fundamental problem he did solve. He designed a system of traction which enabled the horses to walk alongside the grain which was to be cut.

His young son, Cyrus, had watched these experiments and when the old man finally gave up and admitted himself beaten, the son carried on, profiting by his father's experiments and trying to invent the machine that his father had dreamed of. He did not have to wait long for success. In 1831 at the age of twenty-two he made a machine that in a public test cut an entire field of six acres of wheat in a single afternoon. He made some further improvements and in 1832 offered the reaper for sale at fifty dollars each.

The machine bore little resemblance to a modern self binder which had not yet been dreamed of. As the wheat was cut, it fell in orderly rows on a platform and a farm hand who followed the machine raked it to the ground in small piles to be tied into bundles. By all modern standards it was crude and clumsy and poorly constructed, but with it two men and a team of horses could do the work of more than a half dozen men in the harvest field. The rather high price was partly justified by the fact that iron then sold at more than ten cents a pound. All metals were much more expensive than they became later, when advances in metallurgy brought about improved methods of converting and refining. Copper was twenty cents a pound and sheet brass twenty-five to thirty cents.

Each year McCormick cut his own or a neighbor's wheat and each year made improvements on his machine as a result of these field tests. Each year farmers gathered to watch the machine work and exclaimed at the rapidity with which the wheat was harvested, but no one bought a machine. No one actually needed a reaper because the individual wheat fields were too small to utilize one. In order to make efficient use of it, farmers would have to plant larger fields of wheat, and they were haunted by fear of the loss they would suffer if the machine broke down. It was a new contraption which they did not understand and they were not only mystified but a little terrified by it.

Finally in 1840, nine years after he had made his first successful demonstration, Cyrus Hall McCormick sold his first machine. With this encouragement he went to work on an improved reaper which would cut wet grain as well as dry, something the first machine could not do. This new machine was offered for sale at one hundred dollars and sales slowly increased. He sold seven in 1842, twenty-nine in 1843 and fifty the following year. The reaper was talked about all over the country and tales of its performance spread from state to state. The purchaser of one of the early machines set a world record by cutting 175 acres of wheat in one harvest season of eight days. This was equal to the work of two dozen men with cradles.

Other reapers were manufactured and the bitter rivalry of competition stirred up interest and created sales for all the manufacturers. The casual manner in which patents had been granted led to many charges of infringement and years of litigation. Circus-like field tests were held with representatives of rival machines reaping the wheat in different parts of the same field. In one grand tournament of this kind no less than forty machines were entered. They proved to farmers that reapers were practical, just as the now half-forgotten endurance runs which were held the first part of this century demonstrated that motorcars were more than rich men's toys.

Western land put under cultivation created a new demand for reapers. When the gold rush to California left farmers without hired hands, cattle and hogs were turned into thousands of acres of ripe wheat because there were no harvest hands. In a single generation reapers became a necessity. The new barbed wire was largely used to enclose wheat lands in the western plains. A series of improvements made the reaper more efficient and reduced the amount of hand labor. Just before the Civil War the hand who did the raking could be dispensed with, for the wheat was raked off the platform automatically. Later the self binder was perfected, at first binding the bundles with wire and later with twine. With the self binder a man with a team could in one season harvest enough wheat to provide a year's supply of bread for four hundred people. There were sixty thousand reapers of all kinds sold in 1880; a quarter of a million were in use five years later. The machines then in operation were doing the work of five million men. The annual production of wheat was ten bushels per capita instead of four bushels as it had been in 1847. It was probably less than two bushels in colonial days.

At the time young Cyrus McCormick began working on his reaping machine, the methods of separating the wheat from the straw was as primitive as the cutting of the grain with hand sickles. The grain was beaten out by hand. On a windy day it was tossed into the air so that the wind blew the straw and chaff away while the grain fell to the threshing floor. Attempts to make threshing machines were begun about the time the mower inventors started to work and a successful machine was built in 1834. Like the first reaper, it was a crude affair but it did the work that it was intended to do.

For the first time there was bread for everyone in America, good bread at a price everyone could pay. The first mills scattered throughout the country had formerly worked only a few months each year. Now they worked continuously but couldn't keep up with the golden stream of wheat. For more than a dozen years our millers were unable to cope with the flood, and we shipped millions of bushels of wheat to Europe, where it was ground into flour. Fortunately about the time the self binder was perfected a revolution in milling processes sent the old-fashioned millstones on their way to the antique dealers. The new processes used steel rollers, producing as much flour in an hour as the old millstones could grind in a day. The Minneapolis mills, equipped with the new machinery, soon began producing a million barrels yearly. The stream of wheat continued to increase in volume and just a few years later the same mills were exporting a million barrels annually. The cost of turning wheat into flour was reduced to a fraction of what it had formerly been. The old-fashioned miller was accustomed to take one-fourth of the wheat as his toll for grinding. The modern miller, producing thousands of barrels of flour daily, was content with a profit of ten cents a barrel.

Chapter XVIII

THE HOMES ELECTRICITY BUILT

PROFESSOR ALEXANDER GRAHAM BELL exhibited his newly invented telephone at the Centennial Exposition held in Philadelphia in 1876 where it did not attract very much attention, certainly not as much as Daniel Webster's great plow and a whistle someone had fashioned out of a pig's tail. It would have attracted even less but for the fact that Emperor Dom Pedro, of Brazil, personally visited the exhibition because he had been interested in Professor Bell's studies of methods of teaching deaf mutes and had visited his school in Boston. Others followed the royal visitor to the telephone exhibit, but were only casually interested and followed him out again. Some books written about the exposition did not mention the telephone at all. When the inventor tried to interest Boston people in a company to manufacture the new instrument, he found no one willing to invest any money. For sometime thereafter he had to continue to earn his living by delivering lectures in which he explained and demonstrated his invention. It was a novel lecture subject and the attendance was fairly satisfactory.

There was another exhibit at Philadelphia that was also almost entirely overlooked. In an obscure corner a small dynamo buzzed away and from wires attached to some part of the mechanism a strange blue light appeared, lighting up that part of the building even on the darkest days. That was the beginning of the electric light—the carbon arc light which threatened to dominate the field of illuminants until its sister, the incandescent light appeared a few years later. Still another electrical exhibit was an electric motor which ran a small pump.

These unnoticed exhibits were of greater significance than all the other exhibits combined. They demonstrated the connection between electricity and magnetism, just as the Morse telegraph had, but more convincingly. Once this connection was clear to scientists and inventors, it was inevitable that electricity and the manifold uses of electric transmission of power would follow in rapid succession.

In 1876 when Edison was twenty-nine years old very few Americans were interested in electricity. Dr. Franklin's celebrated experiment had been carried out more than a hundred years before this. The telegraph had been invented thirty years before, but after the first flurry of excitement about it had died down, it did not intrude much on the public attention. The public generally looked on it as an adjunct of railway operations sometimes used by the big newspapers. Not many business telegrams were sent and still fewer personal messages. But the few people who were interested in this new application of electricity were intensely interested—the arc lamp people most of all. The kerosene lamp was still something of a novelty, yet a good many fortunes had been made in the oil business and others were piling up rapidly.

The carbon arc light, it was thought, would be equally revolutionary. Here was an illuminant that could be used for lighting streets, buildings, and factories that was as far ahead of gas lighting as the kerosene lamp had been ahead of the old lard oil lamp. The manufacturers did not wait to perfect their small lighting sets before placing them on sale. Salesmen were inexperienced and knew little or nothing about the new product but they broke down consumer resistance by the sheer weight of their own enthusiasm. The representatives of several companies traveled fast and far, selling individual installations to stores and factories and helping local communities organize companies and secure contracts for street lighting. John Wanamaker installed in his store the first electric light in Philadelphia, just as he subscribed to the first telephone. The sidewalk in front of his store was crowded with curious spectators. A newspaper reporter described the new light as "miniature moons or candle points held captive in a glass globe." A little later a San Francisco company was formed which installed lamps and supplied current to local business houses at a flat monthly rate—the first public electric light service in the world. The city of Wabash, Indiana, was lighted with arc lamps on steel towers two hundred feet high. It was said that one could read a newspaper with this light at a distance of a mile. In a surprisingly short time the new lights were installed in Mississippi River steamers as well as in those on Puget Sound. The new lights were not cheap. The San Francisco company started out by charging ten dollars a week for each light but later reduced this to six dollars. The lighting sets were sold as fast as they could be manufactured. The arc lamp manufacturers were in the heyday of success in 1879 when Edison exhibited his new incandescent lamp, and the battle for the electric light business of the country waged furiously for several years. The arc lamp people held a decided advantage in the fact that their lamps used a high voltage of electricity which could be carried long distances without a serious diminution in power. On the other hand, the incandescent lamps used a low voltage which could be carried only a short distance. Lamps connected with the current more than three miles from the central plant did not shine with full brilliancy and were useless at a distance of five miles. When Edison began organizing an electric light service for Manhattan Island he planned several power houses to be located in different parts of the city.

By this time the circle of people interested in these startling new electrical developments had widened. A great many young men who had been planning other careers for themselves turned to the study of electricity and important discoveries were made with a startling rapidity. One of these came early enough to make the new incandescent light available to people living in the suburbs as well as those living in the centers of large cities. It was later to make possible cheap and efficient electric power as well as light to people living in remote farms. This was the transformer, which transforms high voltage current to low. By its use the high voltage current may be sent long distances and then stepped down for local use.

The new incandescent lights, like arc lighting, were not cheap—were, in fact, very dear when compared to present-day rates. The dynamos which generated for current had not reached a high degree of efficiency nor had the steam engines which drove the dynamos. A thousand little economies which together provide savings of great importance were yet to be made.

A comparison of the cost of bulbs sixty years ago with present-day costs will indicate the extent to which mass production accompanied by improved methods of manufacture have brought down the costs of the now universally used electric light. When Edison started making bulbs his cost was more than a dollar each and it was some years before he was able to get it down to forty cents. This was for the

old-fashioned unimproved sixteen-candle power bulb which
is now rarely seen. Eight separate operations were required,
each of them carried out entirely by hand. It required five
hours to pump the air from the bulb and create a vacuum.
A force of a hundred workmen could make three hundred
lamps in a day. It was a long time before the comforts and
conveniences made possible by these marvelous new electrical devices became cheap enough to be commonly used.
Early telephone rates confined the use of telephones to business houses and only those of great size and prosperity, so
that in the early days the possession of a telephone was
almost as good as a credit rating. In 1894 the daytime charge
for a five minute long-distance call between New York and
Chicago was nine dollars, half that much at night.

Only seventy thousand bulbs were produced in 1882 and
a hundred and twenty-five thousand the following year.
That represented the capacity production of the one plant
able to make bulbs. The red hot hair pin was supposed to
burn for several thousand hours before disintegrating, but
there were many complaints about bulbs that lasted only a
few weeks. With costly current and costly and fragile lamps,
the cost of service was naturally high. Incandescent lights
soon replaced gas for street lighting in parts of New York
and the charge was forty-five cents per light nightly. Such a
rate would be considered prohibitive today, but it was then
cheaper than gas. With the older illuminant a small army of
men were required to light the lamps at night and to extin-
guish them in the morning. With electricity all the lights
could be turned on instantly by pulling one switch at the
central power station.

As the use of electric lights grew, all the old stories that had
been told about the dangers of railways and the laying of

gas pipes were revived and slanted from a new angle. It was said that the electricity from wires strung overhead would kill shade trees and that so much electricity in the air was sure to cause a great deal of sickness. The gas men were accused of circulating these stories, perhaps with some justification, for they were very bitter about this new competition against which they could do nothing. One prominent member of the Masons, who was in the gas business, was quoted as saying that he would never set foot inside a lodge that was lighted with electricity. Public sentiment was against the gas companies. They enjoyed the first municipal monopolies and were generally accused of being dictatorial and unreasonable. Gas rates generally were very high. A high quality gas made of resin sold at eight dollars a thousand feet. Coal gas sold at two to three dollars, or about twice present-day rates.

The development of the electric business was accompanied by many discouraging difficulties, for there were thousands of strange new problems to be solved. Insulations were imperfect and there were a great many minor accidents and some serious ones. Edison insisted on having "men of courage" in his plants because on one occasion when the dynamo appeared to be acting queerly the engineers ran out of the plant and the firemen hid under the boilers. But the use of incandescent lighting spread as did the use of the telephone. By 1891 the new plant at Schenectady, New York, was turning out twenty-five thousand bulbs daily and New York was building a plant that would supply current for two hundred thousand lamps. Three years later there were twenty-five hundred electric light companies in the country and two hundred municipally owned plants. It was roughly estimated that the cost of supplying current for a lamp was one cent an hour.

While Edison and his associates were busy on the rapidly growing electric light industry, others were exploring the manifold possibilities of electric power transmission. Soon motors were being installed in mines, mills, and factories all over the country, speeding up production and lessening costs. Two adaptations of power transmission which had the greatest effect on realty values, the architecture of the country, and the lives of the people were elevators and streetcars. The steam elevator had been in use for some time. Cable cars had been built for use in San Francisco, where they are still in operation, because the hills were too steep for horses. Cable cars had later been adopted in New York and other large cities because they were faster than horsecars. The latter jogged along at about four miles an hour. No one could live more than a few miles from his place of employment. The horsecar lines required the maintenance of large stables and the feeding and replacement of horses made the operation very expensive. In 1886 there were twenty-five thousand horsecars in the country and stables for a hundred and twenty thousand horses. The cost of the cable lines with their miles of wire cables and underground channels was excessive, more than three hundred thousand dollars a mile. Neither cable nor horsecars were heated and in the winter passengers buried their feet in the straw which covered the floors of the cars. Streetcar fares were not uniform, but only short trips could be made for five cents.

Steam elevators were also unsatisfactory though a few were installed in buildings not more than four or five stories high. A few mills were eight or nine stories high but no architect dared to design hotels or office buildings of that height. Thus while the lack of cheap and speedy transportation limited the lateral growth of cities the labor involved in climbing stairs made high flats and apartments impractical. The result was the congestion of population even in cities of ten thousand or less. A very large part of the city people lived in tenements. A few wealthy people might maintain country estates, but there were no suburbs.

Suburbs and skyscrapers developed at the same time and neither would have been possible without the application of electricity. Five miles of track for electric cars could be built at the cost of one mile of cable car track. People could travel farther for the same or for less money. Soon the nickel street-car fare became universal. Office and factory workers alike were able to live miles away from their places of employment, out where real estate was comparatively cheap, and they could afford to buy and build their own homes.

Chapter XIX

TOOLS FOR THE HOUSEWIFE

IT IS safe to assume that in the year 1783, and for many years thereafter, any thrifty American housewife could have told at any time just how many pins, needles, and buttons she had in her sewing basket, for articles which are so humble and common now were then both scarce and valuable. It is difficult today to think of an individual pin or an odd button in a sewing basket as being of any more value than scraps of writing paper, but they once were. Pins were specially treasured. There were no pinmakers in the colonies and for some years after we gained our independence we continued to import all of our supplies from England. Pinmaking was a delicate and tedious operation. The head was formed by wrapping a very fine wire around the top of the pin. The other end was sharpened by hand.

Some idea of the cost of pins is indicated by the terms of a prize offered by the Carolina legislature to anyone who would set up a pinmaking establishment in the state. The stipulation was that the pins must be equal in quality to the imported article and be sold at about 7s 6d per dozen, making the individual pin cost about fifteen cents each. That was about the price they sold for until a little more than a hundred years ago. They cost even more in 1812, for the war with England cut off all importation and there were no pinmakers in the United States. While it is doubtful if thorns were ever generally used to pin up clothing, they did take the place of pins for other purposes. Some of the early Massachusetts woolen mills instructed farmers that it was not necessary to make bags to hold the wool brought to the mill. They could wrap the wool in bed sheets pinned together with thorns. One wonders what kind of bed sheets were used to wrap wool, pinned together with thorns!

Needles were not bought in packages but individually. They also were made by hand and it is surprising to find that they cost less than pins. Five cents was an average price for a good needle made of the best Sheffield steel. All needles were much larger than those in general use today, because all of the fabrics were coarse.

Some idea of the cost of buttons may be gained from the figures in old invoices. Brass buttons imported from England cost the importer the equivalent of ten dollars a gross which would probably mean that they would sell at retail for about ten cents each. Pewter buttons were only slightly less expensive. For several decades after we gained independence we continued to import most of our buttons, though some were made in Connecticut. As was true of practically all handmade manufactures, England could undersell us. A great deal of the work was done by silversmith apprentices, for button making was a part of their trade. We did not learn how to roll brass until 1817, although Paul Revere had learned how to roll the more easily worked copper in 1803. Before this time thin sheets of brass were produced by a very slow and clumsy process. Molten brass was poured between two slabs of soapstone or slate set very close together. After the brass hardened, it was cut into strips of the appropriate width, and buttons were punched out by foot power or water power. They were then smoothed and polished by hand.

After learning how to roll brass, our button manufacturers made rapid progress. The thin sheets of brass of uniform thickness could easily be stamped out by machinery as the brass button manufacturers of Waterbury, Connecticut, soon learned. They made machines operated by water power and soon all the operators had to do was to feed in the brass blanks at one end of the machine and watch the buttons fall into bins at the other. A button finally ceased to be a luxury. These early brass rolling mills would look like toys today, for they rolled a ribbon-like strip only as wide as the diameter of a button. It was almost ten years later before we rolled brass in widths large enough for clock parts. Brass buttons which, when carefully polished, had the semblance of gold, were fashionable for more than half a century. The Connecticut manufacturers could not find the right alloy to produce the desired result, and imported experts from England.

Buttons were also made of pewter and the city of Meriden, Connecticut, probably owes its predominant position in the silver business to the fact that the first pewter buttons made in America were produced there in 1794. The manufacture of buttons was followed by that of pewter teapots, then the cheap but showy Britannia ware, to be followed by mass production of silverware. About the time we began making pewter buttons, some New England manufacturers learned how to make "filled ware," that is, cheap jewelry consisting of a shell of silver filled with lead. Buttons made in this way proved very popular for a brief period.

Brass, pewter, horn, ivory, tin and glass buttons held the field until 1822, when men as well as women were electrified by a startling innovation, a button fashion which swept the country and changed the appearance of most of the clothing worn by men and women. Samuel Willotson and his wife hit on the idea of making buttons out of wood and covering them with cloth. This opened up possibilities in the way of tailoring and dressmaking that had never before been dreamed of. Buttons could be made to match a coat or in any contrasting color that fancy might dictate. The two Willotsons were soon swamped with more orders than they could fill and farmed out orders to neighbors after the sweatshop manufacturing system of the period. The business grew rapidly and in ten years they had a thousand families working for them. The business was getting too big for hand production and, in true Yankee fashion, they devised a button-making machine.

About the same time, a machine for the manufacture of pins in one continuous operation was perfected, and in a short time a gross could be bought at less than the cost of a single handmade pin. This pinmaking machine was purely an American invention in spite of the fact that no American had ever learned how to make pins by hand. The United States Patent Office report for the year 1843 had a number of important inventions to record, including the Morse telegraph, but devoted quite a little space to an excited description of the new pinmaking machine. One paragraph of the report read:

"Until a few years since pins were wholly the product of hand labor, which rendered their manufacture a European monopoly—hand labor in the United States being too expensive to compete with the low price of labor in Europe. It has, however, yielded to mechanical ingenuity; and machines in various parts of our country are yielding pins of the best quality in great quantities. These machines in operation appear to be endowed with human instinct, so regular and so perfect are the various operations performed by them. The wire wound on a large reel is put on the machine, and from that time until the pin is delivered, with the head and the point completed, it is not touched by the hand; and although it has to undergo operations of cutting off, forming the head and grinding and polishing the point, the finished pins drop from the machine as fast as if they had to undergo only one of these operations, for the machine is so regulated that the moment one has been cut off it is transferred, as if by instinct, to the next operation which is performed whilst the first operation is repeated on another, and so on to the completion; there being as many pins in the machine as there are operations to be performed, each pin undergoing one operation."

The machine made pins so fast that the hand labor involved in sticking the pins in paper cost more than the pins themselves. A machine to do this was soon invented and a newspaper of 1844 described it in enthusiastic terms:

"A manufactory near Derby, Connecticut, has a contrivance for sticking pins in paper which is quite marvelous. It takes in England the labor of fifty people to stick in one day, by sunlight, ninety packs consisting of 302,960 pins. The same operation is performed here, in the same time, by one woman. Her sole occupation is to pour them, a gallon at a time, into a hopper, from whence they come out all neatly arranged upon their several papers. The mechanism, by which the labor of fifty persons is saved daily, yet remains a mystery to all but the inventor; and no person beyond the single woman who attends it is, upon any pretext whatever, allowed to enter the room where it operates."

The first wire factory had been established at Stamford, Connecticut, in 1825 and the successful drawing of wire led to the manufacture of a great many other sewing basket requisites. Before that time the small amount of wire produced in this country had been made by hammering brass, copper, or iron into slender rods which were then drawn by hand with the use of wooden windlasses. Cheap wire of uniform quality inspired Connecticut manufacturers to attempt to make hooks and eyes. The English imported article had cost $1.50 per gross but by 1836 a Waterbury factory was making them so cheaply that they could be sold at retail for forty cents a gross.

During the first half of last century the sewing basket was a household article of constantly increasing importance. Improvements in textile machinery relieved housewives of the drudgery of spinning, weaving, and dyeing. But as textiles became cheaper and were available in greater variety, the making of clothing demanded more attention. Wardrobes were larger and styles changed more often. The industrious housewife no longer spent hours at the spinning wheel but she wore her needle thin.

The invention of a practical sewing machine might logically have been expected to come from England for, with the sole exception of the cotton gin, we had made no contribution to the development of textiles. But it was purely an American invention. It came into being in the same decade with the machine for making pins and wood screws and in the same part of New England in which these inventions had been conceived. The women did not accept the sewing machine with any more alacrity than the farmers accepted the reaper. It was an imperfect machine and like a great many other American inventions had to wait for further developments both in metallurgy and machine tools before it could be manufactured at a reasonable price. It has been estimated that if the original inventor had been offered a contract to build twelve of the crude machines, the cost would have been at least five hundred dollars each.

Many other patents on improvements were taken out, and one by one the many problems connected with making it a practical machine were solved, but women did not buy them. They were not only expensive but very noisy. A writer of the Civil War period refers to the "nervous grinding of the cams and the harsh clatter of the cogs and gears."

The machine was still noisy, expensive, and inefficient when the Civil War brought a demand by the War Department for a million uniforms. The government contracted for thousands of sewing machines; these were loaned free to sewing circles which worked on the making of uniforms. It was in this way that many thousands of women learned to operate the machine while the manufacturers by mass production methods were able to cut down the cost of manufacture. A commentator of a period shortly after the Civil War said that sewing machines were "now within the reach of every family of thrifty habits." There were thousands of women who were potential customers for sewing machines and installment payment plans made purchases easy. Within ten years American factories were turning out two thousand sewing machines a day—manufacturing sensation of the day.

The sewing machine which is now more widely used by clothing manufacturers than by housewives was the most ambitious of many machines and devices which were made to lighten the work of the housewife. The pump located over the kitchen sink, pumping water from a well beneath the house was the pride of many a housewife—the envy of her neighbors who had to carry water long distances. The sewing machine which had been preceded by the development of cheap textiles made clothing more abundant and also increased the household wash. Several washing machines were patented and placed on sale before the Civil War. One of them, manufactured by Harper Twelvetrees, was exhibited at the London Exposition of 1862 and attracted a great deal of attention. The pictures show it as a wooden box on rockers with a close-fitting lid.

A milking machine was another Yankee marvel of this exposition, but one the urban Londerers declined to take very seriously. They also learned about Maizona, one of the first of the prepared foods which were later to lighten the work of cooking. Maizona, which was a by-product of the starch manufacturers, was served at the exposition and advertised on all the poster boardings of London as "a sort of flour carefully prepared from the finest portions of the maize or Indian corn and so rich in mucilage as entirely to supersede the use of eggs in the preparation of custards and puddings."

This exhibit of American products was not much to look at alongside the rich merchandise and the rare art displays of European countries, but it was typical and representative of that period of our life when the energies of our manufacturers were devoted to the production of machinery which would lighten human labor. The London newspapers, commenting on the washing machine and the milking machine, were amazed at the number of new machines devised for the use of the housewife. One of them said: "Thus we find America producing a machine even to peel apples; another to beat eggs; a third to clean knives; in fact there is scarcely a purpose for which the human hands have been ordinarily employed for which some ingenious attempt is not made to find a substitute in a cheap and efficient labor saving machine."

Very few years elapsed before we were selling those useful tools to housewives in all parts of the civilized world.

Chapter XX

BONES AND SINEW OF INDUSTRY

There were never enough pots and pans, hinges, pot hooks, nails, andirons, chains, and other iron articles to meet the needs of the colonists, and when the long war for independence was ended these items were scarcer than before. Nothing had been imported and the few forges which were in operation had been completely occupied making cannon and other implements of war, including the giant chain which kept the British fleet from control of the Hudson River. There were a great many small forges and blast furnaces scattered about the country, for while the British laws had severely prohibited the manufacture of iron, the colonists had been encouraged to produce pig iron which could be shipped to England duty free. Manufacturing was prohibited. There were very few Americans who knew anything more about the craft of the ironmaster than how to melt iron and run the molten metal off into molds to form pigs of cast iron. During the war they had done their best to supply General Washington's troops, but many of the cannon had burst and some of the bayonets had snapped under the impact of use.

So our great iron and steel industry, which has made all other industries possible, was inaugurated by men who knew practically nothing about the business they were undertaking. Raw materials were plentiful and close at hand. Iron ore was found in bogs and swamps, where it had been deposited as a kind of sediment from iron impregnated water. It was raked out by the use of oyster rakes. In some places it was found lying on the ground. The dense forests provided a supply of charcoal which appeared to be inexhaustible. Oyster shells provided the lime flux needed to do the scavenger work of iron refining until it was discovered that limestone would do the same work better. This discovery greatly widened the field of operations, for forges and furnaces could be set up in dozens of widely separated spots far from a supply of oyster shells.

The early ironmasters who molded pots and skillets and other so-called "hollow ware" operated blast furnaces which brought the iron to a liquid state so that it could be poured into molds. But many other ironmasters used a crude short-cut method of producing iron. They built forges which enabled them to turn the ore into malleable iron bars without actually bringing it to the melting point. The establishments were not unlike the forge of the old-fashioned blacksmith shop in which iron was heated so that it could be hammered into shape on an anvil. They were large enough to hold several bushels of ore, a vast quantity of charcoal, and as much limestone as the ironmaster thought essential. All were piled in together but with the charcoal so arranged as to bring the maximum amount of heat in contact with the flux and the ore. The charcoal fires, fanned by a huge leather bellows, brought the ore to a semi-molten state, though they never liquefied it. Stirring with long iron rods helped to dislodge some of the slag cinders and other impurities.

When the mass of metal was thought to have reached the proper state of malleability, it was drawn from the forge, hammered with sledge hammers or with a trip hammer operated by water power. This operation had the effect of driving out more of the cinders and slag, but some of these impurities always remained even though the mass was always reheated and given a second and sometimes a third hammering. The product was always defective. Some lots were better than others, but the ironmaster seldom knew exactly why.

The firing of one heat of ore comprised a day's work and the output was one hundred and fifty to two hundred pounds. That was about as much as the forge would accommodate and was also as much as a strong man could handle with a pair of tongs. This daily production was often interrupted. Water power was required to operate the bellows and the trip hammer and in winter the water wheel was sometimes encased in ice, while in summer the streams often dried up. In the year 1800 thousands of men were engaged in the smelting of iron but the production for the year was fifty thousand tons—an amount that the blast furnaces of today can produce in one eight-hour shift.

This small production represented the work not only of the men at the forge but of others who were employed quarrying limestone, burning charcoal, and bringing the ore from the swamps or mines. No wonder the bars which were hammered from this lump of iron sold at ten cents or more a pound. The operators of blast furnaces who made pots and kettles and other hollow ware also had to charge a very high price for their wares which frequently cracked and were easily broken.

Some of these early products of the American molders have survived and are to be found on sale in antique shops. The price asked for them often appears to be unusually high, because we instinctively compare them with the prices asked for similar articles today. Actually some of this Americana which is now presumed to have an increased value because of its age and rarity is sold for about the original price. The kitchen equipment of any American home before 1830 consisted of little more than the pots, pans, and kettles that could be used in an open fireplace and the Dutch oven. The articles were heavy, clumsy and crude and one is likely to jump to the conclusion that they were cheap. Actually every one of these articles could be duplicated today in the best aluminum ware at a fraction of the original cost.

The ironmasters cast this hollow ware for the fireplace kitchens, but the principal customers for other products were the country blacksmiths who bought the iron rods and hammered them into hinges, spikes, pot hooks, andirons and other utensils of everyday use. Iron was so expensive that it was not used except where wood was impractical. The heavy timbers of early houses were fastened together with pegs—a building practice that was continued until long after the Civil War. Harrows were made with wooden teeth, while plows and spades were only "shod" with iron.

With their first sale of iron rods to the blacksmith there was established a relationship between the ironmaster and the metal workers that has never changed, and has resulted in the amazing development of the great iron and steel industry of today. Like all other American industries, it differed from those of England and Europe in that it was founded on the customer demand of the common people. The great foundries of England and Europe prospered on government contracts for armaments, while our small forges and furnaces laid the foundation for the greatest industry of them all by catering to the needs of the country blacksmith who in turn supplied the demands of the farmers. The great steel mills are now located far from the farms, but they are still rooted in the soil.

The country blacksmith was the first of the metal workers

Ladies now call them brassieres

Dr. Mason's invention was a boon to those who picked their teeth

Josiah Allen's wife wrote best sellers of her day

The secret of a popular hair-do is revealed

No gas coupons needed for this stylish two wheeler

Popular new gadgets advertised in 1877

Kerosene brought a new luxury in illuminants

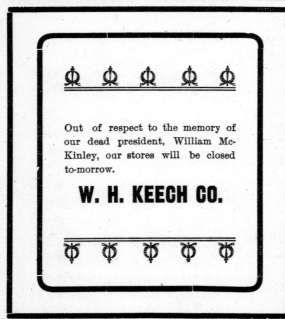
The new Kodak camera is announced, price $25

to turn the products of the ironmaster into saleable merchandise. He constantly demanded better iron, insisted on
what was for several generations thought to be an unattain-
able ideal—iron as good as that produced in England,
Sweden, or Russia. He wanted iron strong enough to be
used in making chains and tires for wagon wheels and he
naturally blamed the ironmaster for any defects in the
articles he hammered out on his anvil. Several generations
of ironmasters had to listen to complaints of their customers,
conscious of the fact that their bars and plates were inferior
to those imported. In fact, people living along the seaboard
bought imported iron and American forges flourished
mainly in the interior, where distance and high transportation costs protected them from this foreign competition.

Aside from the fact that they were more experienced,
there was another practical reason why the ironmasters of
these foreign countries should produce a better product
than the Americans. The iron-producing areas in England,
Sweden, and Russia were restricted. The ore of each country
was of approximately of the same grade, so that a process
which was successful in one section could be used in any
other. This was not true of the many small iron mines which
were worked in New England, Pennsylvania, and New Jersey. Each was different and each presented new problems
which the ironmaster had to solve without the aid of metallurgists.

Improved methods of working iron were introduced, but
without much effect in the way of reduced costs. The first
rolling mills could not, like those of today, roll a lump of
hot iron into a sheet. The making of plates was a long and
laborious and expensive process. The bloom had to be hammered into a rough plate about a half an inch thick. Then

it was heated over a bed of charcoal before being fed into the rollers which reduced the thickness to a quarter of an inch or less. These defective plates, from which the boilers of steam engines were built, cost much more than the boiler plates of today. They may or may not have been entirely to blame for the many boiler explosions that occurred; at any rate Commodore Vanderbilt and the owners of other early steamboat lines were careful to advertise that their boats were equipped with low-pressure boilers.

With each new American invention there was a new and insistent demand for more and better and cheaper iron. A small amount was needed for each of the illegally constructed cotton gins Eli Whitney had invented, and as there were thousands of them the aggregate ran into, for that day, an imposing tonnage. Later Whitney needed iron for his musket factory at New Haven—not only for the fabrication of the muskets but for building the new machines with which the wheels of mass production made their first revolution. Eli Terry and the other Connecticut clockmakers wanted steel good enough to make clock springs like those used by the English clockmakers. Only the English could at that time make this steel and they would sell none of it to us. Terry's generation of clockmakers had to content themselves with weight clocks for which they required many thousand cast-iron weights. McCormick needed good steel for the blades of his reaping machine and got an indifferent quality at a time when steel was selling at eighteen to twenty-five cents a pound, ten times the price at which steel of a superior quality could later be bought.

Many improved methods of producing iron and steel were worked out in England, and news of them reached us in the form of vague rumors which spurred the American iron-

master to new efforts without giving him more than a hint
as to the direction he should take. Metallurgy was then
defined as "the act of extracting metals from their ores" and
was not the exact science it later was to become. Working by
trial and error method the ironmasters did manage to produce a better product, but for a long time their efforts to
make cheaper iron appeared to be frustrated by laws of
nature over which they had no control. The forges and blast
furnaces used vast quantities of charcoal and as the trees in
the immediate vicinity were cut down it became necessary
to go farther and farther afield for supplies, with mounting
costs for transportation. As there were no roads in the forests
the charcoal was carried to the forges in the saddlebags of
horses, a method that was also used to carry ore. The bog ore
began to be exhausted about the same time and the working
of iron mines cost more than delving in the bogs with oyster
rakes. The cost of iron ore at Salisbury, Connecticut, was
five to six dollars a ton. In 1830 pig iron was selling at about
two cents a pound and bar iron for twice that much and
there was little change in price for more than a decade.
Prices, of course, were not uniform, for it was impractical
to transport either pig iron or bars over long distances, and
each forge enjoyed a local market where local prices prevailed. Bars were carried short distances by being bent into
an inverted U shape and thus carried on the backs of horses.
Not only were the prices of iron and steel excessively high
as compared to prices today, but because of their poor quality much heavier weights had to be used to secure the necessary strength. The relative cost of iron and steel products of
a hundred years ago was much greater than the price per
pound would indicate.

About the time the lack of trees from which to make

charcoal appeared to threaten the industry, someone discovered that anthracite could be used in place of charcoal. This was such a surprising discovery that few would believe it until they actually saw the stuff burn. While geologists knew that this hard black rock was actually a kind of superior coal, there were not many geologists in America and they had yet to prove that their profession was a useful one. The practical tests made by an ordinary man were sufficient to prove that this was just a black rock. You could handle it without soiling your hands. You could put it in a grate and burn kindling under it but it would not burst into flames. Obviously just a rock—no matter what the college professors might say. Some people found that when broken into small pieces it made a very satisfactory substitute for gravel and used it for building garden walks. Amateur sculptors chiseled it into curious shapes which they thought to be ornamental.

Ironmasters in Pennsylvania, where the largest deposits of anthracite were to be found, were so certain that charcoal was essential to the industry that they had taken precautions against a shortage. They had bought large tracts of wooded land in the neighborhood of a dam site and an iron mine, establishing what were known as iron plantations. As they believed that charcoal was the only fuel that could be used in blast furnaces, a dependable supply of firewood was considered just as essential as a dependable supply of ore and limestone. The iron plantations had barely been established when recognition of the fact that anthracite was coal made them unnecessary.

The development of steam made possible the use of this new fuel. The charcoal in the furnaces had been fanned by leather bellows, lazily driven by water power. The substitute of steam for water power led to new experiments. Perhaps someone thought of the fact that hot water instead of cold was pumped into boilers of the new steam engines, was struck by the anomaly of pumping cold air into a furnace, and tried the experiment of fanning the flames with hot air. The effect appeared miraculous. This new process had been worked out successfully with charcoal and was found to be equally successful with anthracite.

The ironmasters were apprehensive about the use of this new fuel, just as they had been about the use of limestone instead of oyster shell, but the iron which came from furnaces heated by anthracite was just as good as that produced by charcoal, and the cost was considerably lower. Wood for charcoal had to be cut, then covered with earth and burned, then transported to the furnace. Anthracite could be had for little more than the labor of digging it from the ground. Thus the adoption of the new fuel not only assured a continuous supply of iron but a lower cost of production.

The use of scattered supplies of bog ore soon gave way to the development of iron mines. It was no longer possible for the furnace to be located near both ore and fuel, for it is one of the curious facts of economic geology that deposits of coal and iron are seldom found in the same neighborhood. As it was cheaper to transport ore than coal, it naturally followed that those new furnaces, which were growing larger in size, were located at points where coal rather than ore was plentiful. Coal pits and iron mines were in fixed localities, not scattered and vagrant like bog iron marshes and charcoal kilns. Roads and wagons could be used instead of the piddling and expensive transportation by pack horses.

This change to anthracite came just as railways were being built, and the linking of these two industries was inevitable.

The rapidly expanding railway lines demanded vast quantities of iron and steel—quantities the early ironmasters had never dreamed of, and they helped to make cheap iron possible by providing cheap freight rates for the ore. This marriage of interests which was to have such an effect on American life did not come with the first railways, for our infant iron industry was not prepared to meet their requirements and the railway men went to England for their rails. No single blast furnace was able to fill a large order. In 1840 there were eight hundred of them in operation and the production for the year was less than three hundred thousand tons. We made slow progress in our attempts to become self-sufficient in iron and steel. More furnaces were built and old ones were enlarged but with the growing use of machinery of all kinds demand increased for several generations at a faster rate than production.

Iron was good enough for the country blacksmith shop, but steel was demanded for the new machines whose inventors were crowding the patent office with models. Cast iron was satisfactory for hollow ware, kettles, and pots but was brittle and would break easily. Wrought iron was satisfactory for most of the needs of the blacksmith for it was malleable and would not break like cast iron. Steel was something in between the two—something containing enough carbon to make it hard without becoming brittle. The old process of making it was crude, expensive, and wasteful. After all the carbon possible was extracted from iron bars, they were carbonized again by being heated with powdered charcoal. This was the crude and wasteful method by which an attempt was made to put in exactly the right amount of carbon.

The ironmasters were looking for something to mix with

iron which would more easily convert the metal into steel and while they searched, the material they needed was all about them in the air that they breathed. The discovery that air pumped through the molten iron would burn out impurities was first made by William Kelly, a Kentucky ironmaster, who specialized in making kettles for boiling maple syrup. According to popular legend, the discovery was an accident. In simple terms, he had discovered that if a blast of air is passed through a mass of molten iron, the carbon in the iron burns itself out, supplying its own fuel. Thus the blast of cold air actually raises the temperature of the metal instead of decreasing it. To a people who blew on their coffee to cool it, this idea appeared so utterly absurd that Kelly's friends and his young wife thought he was crazy and had him examined by a physician. Nevertheless he continued to refine iron by this process, though he didn't bother to take out a patent.

In the meantime, in England, Henry Bessemer, who had several useful inventions to his credit, was also working on methods to improve the production of iron and also, it is said, discovered the process by accident. Whereas ironmasters in America had scoffed at Kelly, those of England adopted the Bessemer ideas with enthusiasm. Bessemer promptly invented a converter which made his discovery practical. Kelly contested the granting of an American patent to Bessemer and the new process was not used here until after the Civil War. The age of iron had started in the remote prehistoric past, but the age of steel was conceived in Kelly's discovery of 1846, and born in the period of the Civil War.

The cheaper cost of steel made possible by this process, and the open hearth process which followed it, helped to speed up the building of railways and the improvement of the older roads. "The Bessemer process," as it came to be called, shortened and simplified the process and made the cost of steel just a little more than that of pig iron. In 1867 only about three thousand tons were produced. In 1873 the production was 157,000 tons. It was all eagerly gobbled up by the railways, for in the year just preceding this America had laid seven thousand miles of tracks. In 1850 the cost of producing a ton of pig iron was about eighteen dollars. During the war the cost doubled, but with the return of peace it dropped to twenty-four and later to eleven dollars. These reductions in cost were accomplished in spite of constantly increasing wage scales. By 1892 the production of steel made by this process was more than four million tons. Such a vast amount of steel would have completely swamped the facilities of the earlier rolling mills, but the few decades following the Civil War brought amazing advantages in the efficiency of all steel-making machinery. By 1890 a plant employing only seventeen men could turn out a six-hundred pound rail every thirty seconds. Another plant produced a mile of rails every working day.

It would be difficult to exaggerate the effect that cheap steel has had on the lives of the American people. Every tool from the carpenter's screw driver to the most complicated turret lathe in the machine shop could be produced of better material and at cheaper cost. Steel rails, which quickly replaced the dangerous old iron rails, made it possible to operate heavier trains faster and at reduced costs which were eventually reflected in reduced freight rates. Skyscrapers, apartment houses, and ocean liners became possible.

Metallurgists assumed new duties. They produced steel to meet special mechanical requirements, giving manufac-

turers a scope of action that they had not dreamed of.
Inventors had a new material to work with. Fascinating and
important as it has been, the story of steel has only begun.
New uses for steel are being developed every year.

Chapter XXI

A MILLION DOLLAR HOBBY

GREAT things developed from the fact that twenty-three-year-old George Eastman, who loved music and pictures and an outdoor life, was bored by the routine work as bookkeeper in a Rochester savings bank. In attempts to find relief from the tedious and uninteresting work, he tried to learn to play a flute, without much success, took dancing lessons, rode horseback, and enjoyed zestful vacations. After hours he worked in the small carpenter shop he had established in his mother's home, producing the hideous scroll saw work which in the Centennial year was exerting a strange fascination on Americans of all degrees and putting a blight on American architecture. By all the success formulas of the period, young Eastman should have settled down to the job of bank bookkeeping where a fortune made along safe and conventional lines most certainly awaited him. His temperament and talents appeared to make a career of this sort inevitable. He had saved a part of the first money he ever earned, had invested five hundred dollars in a mortgage bond before he came of age, and now at the age of twenty-three had more than three thousand dollars in cash and securities. The money had been accumulated by careful and systematic savings rather than by parsimonious hoarding. He had always contributed to the Sunday School, spent money on candy and figs for himself and flowers for his girl friends.

The attempts to play a flute, the scroll saw work, and the horseback rides did not relieve the ennui of the hours spent on a bookkeeper's stool, and he finally took up a hobby—photography—becoming the first amateur photographer in the world. It was an expensive hobby. The first equipment he bought involved an outlay of almost a hundred dollars and there was a constant expense for chemicals, plates, and other supplies. He also had to arrange for lessons from a local photographer in what was known as "the art of photography."

The art was complicated and difficult and the paraphernalia heavy and cumbersome. Even in a properly equipped studio the photographer had to mess about with stuffy dark rooms, coat the plates with collodion and nitrate of silver, make the exposure, and then develop the plate before the coating dried. The young amateur multiplied all of the difficulties of studio photography because all the pictures he made were out-of-doors and he had to carry the equipment with him.

"I bought an outfit and found that it took not only a strong but a dauntless man to be an outdoor photographer," Eastman later recalled. "My layout, which included only the essentials, had in it a camera about the size of a soap box, a tripod, which was strong and heavy enough to support a bungalow, a big plateholder, a dark tent, a nitrate bath and a container for water. . . . Nitrate of silver had to go along and it was perhaps the most awkward companion possible on a journey. Being corrosive, the container had to be of glass and the cover tight, for silver nitrate is not a liquid to get intimate with. The first time that I took a silver bath away with me, I wrapped it with exceeding great care and put it in my trunk. The cover leaked, the nitrate got out and stained most of my clothing."

Loaded down with this heavy equipment, Eastman spent

all fair weather holidays traveling about the countryside photographing scenes that interested him, just for the fun of it. He had no idea of going into the photographic business. Nor did he think of giving up his position in the bank where he was earning what was for his age and for that period the remarkably high salary of fourteen hundred dollars a year. But his interest in amateur photography increased, and soon he was reading everything he could find on the subject. Learning that some good photographic journals were published in French and German, he bought dictionaries and textbooks, engaged a teacher, and began studying those languages. In one of the journals he read of a method by which plates could be coated with a sensitized gelatine emulsion and used when dry. The process had been worked out by a professional photographer in England, but was not in general use. Doubtless hundreds of professional photographers in America read about this process and promptly forgot about it. They worked in studios where the preparation of wet plates was an old established routine which they had mastered and they did not want to take the time to learn the new method. But to the young amateur, who had to lug his heavy apparatus through the country, the idea of dry plates was absorbing. It meant that he could coat his plates at home, go into the country accompanied only by his camera. The dark tent and the troublesome silver nitrate could be left at home.

The English formula was tedious and troublesome, but it did produce successful dry plates and provided a starting point for the experiments the young bank clerk carried on until late every night. He had started solely with the idea of making dry plates for his own convenience, but as he solved one problem after another, and saw success just ahead, he began to see that there might be commercial possibilities in the sale of dry plates. He was sure of it when he had completed his experiments, because he had not only improved the original formula for dry plates but had invented a machine which would do the coating and produce a more uniform coating than was possible by hand methods.

In three years after Eastman took up the hobby of amateur photography, he had secured both British and American patents on his process for making dry plates and was in the business of supplying plates to professional photographers. He had greatly reduced the cost of photography and the dry plates provided a great convenience for the small but growing number of amateurs. To a man of less vision it might have appeared that the demands of the market had been satisfied. Up to that time the successful American manufacturers were those who had supplied their fellow Americans with necessities. The photo studio where family portraits were made might possibly have been classed as a necessity but supplies for amateur photographers who tramped about the country taking pictures for the fun of it could not be placed in that category. There were not in fact enough amateur photographers to provide business for one photo supply shop, and Eastman was one of the very few men who believed that thousands of people would eventually adopt photography as a hobby. He had found pleasure in taking pictures when it was both laborious and expensive. He set himself now to the task of making it easy and cheap.

The photo films were the first step and these were in production in 1884. Three years later the first Kodak appeared, a faulty and expensive instrument compared with its successors. In appearance it was much like the box type "Brownie" which was sold fifty years later. It was light enough to be held in the hand while making an exposure. The picture made was a circle two and a half inches in diameter. The camera came loaded with a strip of film which would take one hundred pictures. The price was twenty-five dollars. When the hundred pictures had been taken the camera had to be sent to the Eastman establishment in Rochester where the exposed film was developed and printed and a new film placed in the Kodak at a charge of ten dollars. Amateur photography was safely launched as an American hobby which was soon to become international. Eastman advertised it extensively in all the good magazines, and soon millions were familiar with his slogan:

"You Press the Button. We do the Rest."

New models of the Kodak followed in rapid succession, each one embodying some improvement not found in its predecessor. By 1891 the new Kodak could be loaded in daylight. Rolls of film could now be bought anywhere and it was unnecessary to ship the instrument to Rochester to be serviced. The first of the small photographic shops which were soon to dot the country and now number more than seventy thousand began to appear. There was an avalanche of orders and so many people began carrying Kodaks and pressing the button that the Chicago *Tribune* referred to the hobby as a "craze" which, it said, "was spreading fearfully." The papers were full of Kodak jokes which were as common but more kindly than the Ford jokes a half century later. The hobby spread to England, where Eastman had a factory. Rudyard Kipling bought a Kodak and wrote a letter of appreciation. In Gilbert and Sullivan's comic opera *Utopia* there was a chorus of Kodak girls and two of them sang a song in which the following stanza occurred:

"Then all the crowd take down our looks
In their pocket memorandum books
To diagnose
Our modest pose
The Kodaks do their best.
If evidence you would possess
Of what is maiden bashfulness,
You only need a button press
And we will do the rest."

In 1896 the hundred thousandth Kodak was made. There were then a number of models on the market. The folding Kodak had been made; also other models which sold for twelve dollars and five dollars. It is an interesting coincidence that the Eastman models followed exactly the same scale of price reductions as Eli Terry's clocks, which first sold at twenty-five dollars, then twelve and then five dollars. A cartridge of film containing twelve exposures sold for ninety cents but as the large quantities manufactured brought down the cost of production, the price was reduced to sixty cents.

With the completion of his first Kodak Eastman launched an advertising campaign which was sensational not only in its volume but in its international scope. He not only bought large space advertisements in the best American magazines but signed a three-year contract for the best space on the bus lines of Paris. His own country as well as England and a good part of the continent of Europe turned to amateur photography almost between one week-end and another—certainly with much more rapidity than Eastman had any reason to expect, but he never relaxed his advertising which created more customers. Customers meant greater production. Greater production meant decreased cost in the unit of manufacture. With each decrease in the cost of Kodaks and films the number of people who could afford to became amateur photographers increased until they now number about twenty million in the United States alone. And so the pump priming of advertising built up a constantly increasing demand for Kodaks and films not only in the United States but all over the world.

George Eastman's attempt to build a hobby into an industry probably would not have succeeded as it did a generation or even a decade earlier. The era of novelty was setting in when he became an amateur photographer. People who had gone to the Centennial Exposition at Philadelphia, had seen the telephone Mr. Bell had invented. They had also seen the electric motor, dynamo, and arc light, though they had not paid much attention to them. Picture post cards and that new French invention, the cigarette, had attracted more attention than those new electrical gadgets which were so soon to transform the world in which we live.

Other things were happening to impress on Americans the conception of a new age of things that were different. Paper collars for men were put on sale to be followed by paper cuffs and shirt fronts and paper collars for ladies. There was a brief vogue for steel collars and steel shirt fronts enameled white in imitation of linen, guaranteed to be impervious to moisture and easily cleaned with a damp cloth. New York was excited about the project of a well-known engineer for a pneumatic railway which was not a railway. It was a huge tube in which passengers and freight enclosed in great hollow balls would be shot through the tubes by compressed air.

Another change in American life which helped the sale of amateur cameras and other Eastman products was the bicycle. Having conquered the forest by destroying it, the frontiersman looked on the road between his home and the county seat as nothing more than a difficult route to be negotiated as infrequently as possible. The grandsons of the pioneer who had white-collar jobs in the county seat stuck there until the bicycle sent them from the cities and towns to rediscover the beauties of the country life their grandfathers had enjoyed. As soon as Kodaks of the smaller lighter models appeared on the market, cyclists began to carry them. It must be remembered that until comparatively recent years the Kodak was purely an outdoor camera. The bicycle and the Kodak flourished together, made town-dwelling people conscious of the beauties of the country life, and helped to create a demand for better roads.

Chapter XXII

A CENTURY AND A HALF OF PROGRESS

1780 First hat factory started by Zadock Benedict in Danbury, Connecticut. He boasted that he could turn out three hats a day.

1788 Hartford Woolen Mills organized.

1790 First census showed country had a population of 3,929,214

1793 Eli Whitney invented the cotton gin which would do the work of ten men.

1794 Wheat cradle began to replace the old hand sickle. Congress passed bill establishing an arsenal at Springfield, Massachusetts.

1795 Jacob Perkins of Newburyport, Massachusetts, was granted a patent for a nailmaking machine. The United States government agreed to pay tribute to the Dey of Algiers for "protection" from the Algerian pirates. Etienne Boré developed an improved method for extracting sugar from cane.

1796 John Fitch ran the first steamboat on a small lake in New York City. Major Isaac Craig and Colonel James O'Hara established the first glass works in Pittsburgh.

1797 First salt factory established in Ohio. First machine for making combs patented by Isaac Tyrone. First American sailing ship launched on Lake Erie. Merino sheep smuggled out of Spain and brought to the United States.

1799 First shipment of ice from New York to Charleston, South Carolina. Eliakim Spooner secured patent for a seeding machine. Samuel Slater established first cotton mill and Sunday School.

1800 Second census gave population of the country as 5,308,483. Eli Whitney introduced mass production by manufacturing muskets with interchangeable parts. First rubber ever seen in the United States brought to Boston.

1801 First sheet copper rolled at Paul Revere's mill at Canton, Massachusetts.

1802 Process for making potato starch in large quantities patented by John Biddle of Philadelphia. First large powder factory established by I. Du Pont. Abel Porter began the manufacture of gilt buttons in Connecticut.

1803 First patent for reaping machine issued. New Hampshire's first cotton mill built.

1804 Machine embroidering introduced by John Duncan. Middlesex Canal connecting Boston and Concord River completed. Samuel Wetherill began the manufacture of white lead at Philadelphia. First bananas imported into the United States.

1805 First drove of cattle crossed the Alleghenies for the eastern slaughter houses. Printers' ink manufactured in New York.

1806 First confectionery established in New York City. David Melville of Newport, Rhode Island, lighted his house with gas. First American saws manufactured by William Rowland of Philadelphia.

1807 Robert Fulton's steamboat, the *Clermont*, made the trip from New York to Albany. Patent shot tower built on the Schuylkill. Eli Terry began the manufacture of clocks by machinery. A machine invented for the simultaneous heading and cutting of tacks.

1808 The *Phoenix*, first steamboat to travel at sea, made the trip from New York to Philadelphia. Flint glass manufactured at Pittsburgh.

1809 First duck cloth for sail-making woven in the United States. Abel Stowell of Worcester, Massachusetts, patented a machine for cutting screws.

1810 The census showed the country to have a population of 7,239,881. First metallic pens made by Peregrine Williamson, of Baltimore.

1811 First steamboat left Pittsburgh for New Orleans by way of the Ohio and Mississippi Rivers. Steam ferry between Hoboken and New York established. Francis Cabot Lowell went to Manchester to study textiles. He was not allowed to make drawings.

1812 Pins made in the United States for the first time. First rolling mill built in Pittsburgh. National City Bank established.

1813 The manufacture of hair cloth began at Rahway, New Jersey. First mill in the world capable of turning raw cotton into finished cloth established at Waltham, Massachusetts. Printing from stereotyped plates introduced.

1814 Steel plate engraving invented by Jacob Perkins of Newburyport, Massachusetts, who had previously invented a nail-making machine.

1815 Steam power first used in furniture factory. First steamboat ascended the Mississippi to Louisville.

1816 Streets of Baltimore illuminated by gas. First savings bank in the country established at Philadelphia. American Bible Society organized.

1817 Ground broken for construction of the Erie Canal. Steam power first used in paper making. Harper publishing house founded.

1818 Elisha Mills began the packing industry at Cincinnati. Internal revenue tax on whiskey abolished. Steam packet line between New York and New Haven established.

1819 John Conant of Vermont invented the cooking stove which slowly replaced the fireplace. The *Savannah*, first steamship to cross the Atlantic, left port May 21 and reached Liverpool June 20. Plow with interchangeable parts invented by Jethro Wood. Ezra Daggett and Thomas Kensett start first canning plant in New York.

1820 Census gives population of the country as 9,634,453. First steamboat on Lake Michigan. Thomas Blanchard patented the gunstock lathe. First crushed stone road built.

1821 Miss Sophia Woodhouse of Weatherford, Connecticut, patented a straw hat made of the native grasses.

1822 Mason & Baldwin of Philadelphia began engraving cylinders for calico printing. First patent for artificial teeth granted to C. M. Graham. Iron conduit pipes used for the first time in Fairmount Water Works, Philadelphia. Luke Davies of New York opened the first store devoted exclusively to men's furnishing goods.

1823 First steam power printing press set up in Albany. Champlain Canal connecting the Hudson River and Lake Champlain opened.

1824 Isinglass manufactured at Cape Cod. Glazed ground wall papers first made.

1825 Erie Canal completed after seven years of work, opened with grand celebration in New York. Isaac Babbitt of Trenton, Massachusetts, invented Babbitt metal, an alloy of tin and copper. Porcelain manufactured at Philadelphia.

1826 First railway with metal rails at stone quarry near Quincy, Massachusetts. Power loom for weaving wire invented by John S. Gastrine. Manufacture of palm leaf hats begun in Massachusetts. W. Kendall patented insertable teeth for circular saws. First cylinder press.

1827 Sandwich Glass Company made first compressed glass. First drove of hogs brought to Chicago packing plant. First issue of *Youth's Companion*.

1828 First edition of Webster's Dictionary published. William Woodworth of Hudson, New York, invented first machine for cutting tongues and grooves in lumber. First mass production of axes begun by Samuel Collins in Connecticut.

1829 Manufacture of sewing silk by machinery begun by James Conant at Mansfield, Massachusetts. Dr. John M. Revere perfected the process for making galvanized iron. First paper made from grass and straw fiber by machinery by G. A. Shyrock at Philadelphia. The Stourbridge Lion, first locomotive to run in America, arrived from England.

1830 The fifth census showed population of the country to be 12,866,020. Joseph Dixon began the manufacture of lead pencils. Baltimore and Ohio opened the first section of railway operated by horsepower. Sheet brass rolled at Waterbury, Connecticut. First American locomotive constructed by Peter Cooper. First telescope used in United States for astronomical purposes. Race between train and horse at Baltimore.

1831 First train drawn by a locomotive ran on the South Carolina Railroad. Timothy Barclay of Albany invented power loom for stocking weaving. Baldwin Locomotive works established in Philadelphia.

1832 First street railway in the country opened in New York between City Hall and Fourteenth Street. First soda water apparatus manufactured by John Matthews of New York. Wholesale clothing factory established in New Haven. First shirt factory in New York.

1833 First cargo of American ice shipped to India. Obed Hussey patented and exhibited a successful reaping machine. New York *Sun* founded. Samuel Preston invented a machine for pegging shoes.

1834 Cyrus Hall McCormick secured patent on his reaper. First oil crushed from cotton seed. Screws first made entirely by machinery. Manufacture of door locks began in Connecticut.

1835 Pins first made by machinery in New York. Samuel Colt began the manufacture of the "revolving pistol." Horseshoes made by machinery. Professor H. B. Morse exhibited his telegraph at the University of New York.

1836 First patent of friction match granted to Alonzo D. Phillips of Springfield, Massachusetts. Manufacture of fine cut chewing tobacco begun in Mississippi. First sleeping car run on Cumberland Railway. First American patent issued for a typewriting machine. Rubber belting patented.

1837 Canning of sweet corn begun by Thomas B. Smith at Philadelphia. Pitts brothers patented the combined threshing and cleaning machine. Brass generally adopted for clock manufacture.

1838 Elisha H. Root of Collinsville, Connecticut, invented machine for punching eyes in axes and hatchets. First shipment of wheat from Chicago. David Bruce, Jr., invented type casting machine.

1839 First express service started by W. F. Herndon between Boston and New York. Hot water heating introduced in New York.

1840 Population of the country 17,069,453. Patent for electric telegraph issued to Professor Morse. James Chickering patented the grand piano with full iron frame. First mill for drawing brass wire built by Edwin Hodges at West Torrington, Connecticut. The American buggy came into general use.

1841 Canning of salmon began in Maine. First steam fire engine built and used in New York. India rubber ball patented by Edwin Chaffee. Samuel Slocum invented machine for sticking pins in paper. Dun & Bradstreet established.

1842 First attempt made to invent sewing machine. Thomas Kingsford discovered and perfected process of making starch for commercial uses from corn. First factory for pocket knives established in Connecticut.

1843 Patent issued to Enos Widler for first waterproof safe. First chicken eggs in America hatched by artificial heat.

1844 Telegraph messages sent between Baltimore and Washington. Fishing nets woven by machinery. U. A. Boyden built first turbine water wheel for a cotton mill at Lowell, Massachusetts. Patent granted to Charles

Goodyear for method of vulcanizing rubber. Philander Derby designed the Boston rocker.

1845 Telegraph line between Baltimore and Washington opened to public business. Machinery first used in the making of confectionery. Power loom for ingrain carpets invented by Erastus B. Bigelow.

1846 Elias Howe, Jr., patented the first sewing machine. Oliver R. Chase of Boston built first machine for making lozenges. Eastern Hotel in Boston first public building to be heated by steam. Richard Hoe invented new press.

1847 G. Page invented the revolving disc harrow. William Kelly decarbonized iron by blasts of air—the Bessemer process.

1848 Henry P. Westcott invented machine for punching wooden shoe pegs. First cast-iron building in the world erected in New York. First elastic web mill making goring for gaiters.

1849 Improved steam engine invented by George H. Corliss.

1850 Population of the country 23,191,876. Project for transcontinental railway discussed in Philadelphia. S. S. Putnam of Neponset, Massachusetts, began the manufacture of nails for horseshoes by machine. First patent issued for machine to make ice. Machinery first used in the manufacture of shoes. There were 680 American whaling ships.

1851 Hudson River Railroad completed from New York to Albany. Canal from Evansville, Indiana, to Lake Erie completed. The McCormick reaper created a sensation at London Exposition.

1852 First ready mixed paints are offered for sale. Federal

law requires maker's name to be stamped on all boiler plates. Plate glass works started in Brooklyn.

1853 Company organized to lay cable from New York to London. Otis Tufts patented an elevator for hotels. First marble soda fountain creates a sensation in Boston.

1854 The Pennsylvania Railroad completed the tunnel under the Allegheny Mountains. First commercial flour mill established at Minneapolis.

1855 Cottonseed oil first successfully produced by Paul Aldridge at New Orleans. Hugh Borgess patented chemical wood pulp.

1856 First street railway in New England connected Boston and Cambridge. Gail Borden patented process for making condensed milk and began manufacture at Litchfield, Connecticut.

1857 First attempt to lay Atlantic cable unsuccessful. Tea from Japan first appeared on the market. Some states passed laws to prohibit collecting cottonseed. Machine made to sew soles on shoes.

1858 E. S. Drake sank first petroleum well at Titusville, Pennsylvania. Atlantic cable successfully laid. First cut loaf sugar made in the United States.

1859 First shipment of flour from Minnesota to the East. Moses G. Farmer invented the dynamo which replaced the galvanic battery.

1860 Population of the country 31,443,321. Centrifugal machine introduced in sugar refineries. Chain of railways from Bangor, Maine, to New Orleans completed.

1861 Telegraph service opened between St. Louis and San Francisco. Stereotyping for newspapers introduced by *Tribune* and *Herald* in New York. McKay sewing machine for shoes patented. Six shoemakers using old methods could make fifteen pairs of shoes in one day.

1862 First export shipment of American kerosene. Union Pacific Railroad chartered.

1863 Henry Disston built first crucible steel melting plant for saw steel. More than three million slaves freed by Emancipation Proclamation. Ebenezer Butterick sold paper patterns for dressmaking—instant success.

1864 George M. Pullman built his first sleeping car. Northern Pacific Railroad chartered. Postal money order system established.

1865 First rail laid on the Union Pacific. Polished plate glass made at Lenox, Massachusetts. First newspaper press built to print from a continuous roll.

1866 Salmon canned on the Columbia River. Second Atlantic cable successfully laid. Convention of workingmen demands an eight-hour day. Steinway and Company introduced the upright piano. First adding machine placed on the market.

1867 First steel rails rolled at Johnstown, Pennsylvania. Ground wood pulp first used in making paper. First shipment of California fruit received in New York. Pullman Parlor Car Company organized.

1868 First open hearth furnace built at Trenton, New Jersey. Improved typewriter patented by C. Luther Sholes. Westinghouse air brake used successfully.

1869 First transcontinental railway completed. Great Niagara suspension bridge opened. Celluloid invented and made in United States by J. W. and I. S. Hiatt.

1870 Population of the country 39,818,440. Bigelow attacher and heeling machine introduced in shoe factories.

Terra cotta first generally used in buildings. Refrigerator cars first used.

1871 R. Hoe and Company complete the perfecting press. Texas and Pacific railway incorporated. Ship canal across the Isthmus of Panama reported feasible.

1872 First practical use made of the band saw. First iron tanks used to transport oil. Water gas process patented.

1873 Westinghouse automatic airbrake introduced on railways. Apparatus for hot soda water patented.

1874 Eads Bridge across the Mississippi at St. Louis completed. Manufacture of barbed wire begun at De Kalb, Illinois.

1875 First typewriting machine offered for sale. Natural gas first used as a fuel in factory.

1876 Alexander Graham Bell secured patent on telephone. First exportation of dressed beef. Charles Goodyear process of welt sewing perfected.

1877 Colonel A. A. Pope built the first American made bicycle. Bell successfully tested telephone between Boston and Salem, Massachusetts. Talking machine invented by Thomas A. Edison.

1878 First train ran on New York elevated railway. Incandescent lights introduced by Thomas A. Edison.

1879 Beef canning on a large scale introduced by packing houses. First breech loading rifle invented. Cleveland illuminated by electricity.

1880 Population of the country 50,155,783. Edison built first electric road at Menlo Park. First commercial installation of electric lights in an Oregon steamboat.

1881 Germany and France prohibit the importation of American pork.

1882 Machine for stuffing horse collars patented by William

Fogelsang. National Wholesale Druggists Association organized.

1883 Fish canneries for Alaska salmon established. Last spike driven in Northern Pacific Railroad. Brooklyn Bridge opened.

1884 Telephone wires first put under ground. National Confectioners Association of the United States organized. First skyscraper—ten stories—built in Chicago.

1885 Long distance telephone service introduced. Oil fields discovered at Lima, Ohio. Linotype patented by Ottmar Mergenthaler.

1886 Wire nails first manufactured. First oil-tank steamers built.

1887 Beet sugar successfully produced in Colorado. First vestibule Pullman train in service.

1888 First electric street railway built by Frank J. Sprague at Richmond, Virginia. Bell telephone patents confirmed by United States Supreme Court.

1889 Mass production methods in production of window glass introduced by J. Chambers at Jeannette, Pennsylvania.

1890 Population of the country 62,947,714.

1891 First railway passenger train ran to the summit of Pike's Peak. First armor plate supplied to the government by an American mill. Mussel shell buttons made at Muscatine, Iowa.

1892 Long distance telephone line between New York and Chicago formally opened. American locomotive attained speed of ninety-seven miles an hour. First gasoline driven motorcar operated by C. A. Duryea. First Ingersoll dollar watches made.

1893 World's Fair opened at Chicago by President Cleveland. Motion picture projector patented by Thomas A. Edison.

1894 Launching of the *St. Louis*, largest ship ever built in America.

1895 The iron and steel industry set new records in production. Electrification of New York, New Haven and Hartford railway begun.

1896 Professor Langley's model of a flying machine sustained itself in the air and flew a half mile.

1900 Population of the country 75,994,575.

1901 United States Steel Corporation organized by J. P. Morgan & Co.

1902 American factories produced 9,000 motor cars of all types.

1903 Wright Brothers made successful airplane flight at Kitty Hawk, North Carolina.

1904 Government printing office at Washington completely equipped with Mergenthaler linotype. Invention of vacuum tubes for radio. United States auto registration 22,830. Only one hundred and fifty miles of good roads in United States. First successful bottle-making machine patented.

1905 Lewis and Clark Exposition opened at Portland, Oregon. Pennsylvania Railroad announced eighteen-hour service between New York and Chicago.

1906 Ground broken for the steel city of Gary, Indiana. Airplane patents issued to Wilbur and Orville Wright.

1907 Three-electrode vacuum tubes patented by Lee De Forest. First steel sleeping car exhibited at Jamestown exposition.

1908 Andrew Carnegie told Congress the American steel industry no longer needed a protective tariff.

1909 Process of making plastics (Bakelite) invented by Leo H. Bakeland. Wireless messages sent between New York and Chicago.

1910 Population of the country 91,972,266. Ten thousand electric refrigerators sold in the United States at average price of six hundred dollars.

1911 Roosevelt Dam in Arizona completed at cost of $3,-890,000.

1912 Self starter for automobiles offered for sale.

1913 Oil cracking process patented by William M. Barton.

1914 Panama Canal formally opened. Wireless telephone used commercially. Henry Ford announced minimum wage of five dollars for an eight-hour day.

1915 Transcontinental telephone service established. Henry Ford made his millionth car.

1916 America's production of gasoline exceeded that of kerosene. Adoption by United States of first portable air-cooled machine gun.

1917 Price of wheat on the Chicago Board of Trade reached two dollars a bushel for the first time since the administration of President Washington.

1918 Aerial mail service between New York and Chicago established.

1919 Electricity began to be used in household appliances.

1920 Population of the country 105,710,620. An analysis of the figures shows that the number of those living on farms had dwindled to less than thirty per cent.

1921 Radios offered for sale to general public.

1922 Electric clothes washers sold at average price of $153.69.

1923 United States exports of iron and steel amounted to about ten million tons, exceeding that of any other country except Germany.

1924 More than eighteen million telephones in the United States—as many as in all the rest of the world.

1925 American manufacturers adjust themselves to a new system of "hand to mouth" buying made necessary by rapid changes in styles and introduction of new merchandise.

1926 With the increased efficiency of machines, the American worker now produces annually $7,500 worth of merchandise.

1927 Consumption of rayon in the United States now exceeds that of silks.

1928 Boulder Canyon project initiated—great power plant begun.

1929 Major moving picture theatres begin the production of "talking" pictures.

1930 Population of the country is 122,774,046.

1931 Motorcar registration in the United States is 23,059,262.

1932 Rapid change from street railways to motor buses shown by the fact that more than ten thousand miles of streetcar tracks had been abandoned since 1917. George Washington Bridge in New York opened.

1933 The American motion pictures by publicizing the latest styles killed the sale for obsolete clothing in backwoods towns and created a market which demands the same goods in Hick Center as on Fifth Avenue.

1934 The daily newspapers of the United States had a combined circulation of more than forty million copies.

1935 American production of bakery products, exclusive of crackers, amounts to more than one billion dollars.

1936 Commercial production of 100-octane gas begun.

1937 Air conditioning for private home advertised. Glass

skillets placed on the market. Golden Gate Bridge, San Francisco completed.

1938 Approximately twenty-four million homes and five million autos equipped with radios.

1939 Among many new products are paper made from cotton stalks and airplanes made from plywood.

1940 Population of the country 131,669,275. American military plane develops a speed of more than five hundred miles an hour.

1940 Small "camera size" portable radio receiving sets placed on sale.

1941 Survey shows Americans own more than fifty million radio receiving sets.

BIBLIOGRAPHY

ACKERMAN, CARL W. *George Eastman*, New York, Houghton Mifflin Co., 1830.

ALFORD, L. P. *Henry Laurence Gantt, Leader in Industry*, New York, Harper & Brothers, 1934.

BOYD, THOMAS. *Poor John Fitch*, New York, G. P. Putnam Sons, 1935.

BURLINGAME, ROGER. *March of Iron Men*, New York, Charles Scribner's Sons, 1940.

BURLINGAME, ROGER. *Engines of Democracy*, New York, Charles Scribner's Sons, 1940.

CANDLER, HENRY E. *A Century and One*, New York, G. P. Putnam Sons, 1933.

CASSON, HERBERT N. *Cyrus Hall McCormick*, Chicago, A. C. McClurg & Co., 1909.

CLARK, VICTOR S. *History of Manufacturers in the United States*, (three volumes), New York, McGraw-Hill Book Co., 1929.

CASSELL'S ILLUSTRATED EXHIBITOR (The International Exhibition of 1862) London, Cassell, Peter & Galpin. 1862

CONNECTICUT, (*State Guide Series*), Boston, Houghton Mifflin Co., 1938.

DOTY, LOCKWOOD L. *History of Livingston County*. (New York) Genesee, 1876.

DOWNS, JOSEPH. *A Handbook of the American Wing*, New York, Metropolitan Museum of Art, 1942.

DOW, GEORGE FRANCIS. *Domestic Life in New England in the Seventeenth Century*.

DAY, CLIVE. *A History of Commerce*, New York, Longmans, Green & Co., 1914.

DEPEW, CHAUNCY M. *One Hundred Years of American Commerce*, New York, D. O. Haynes & Co., 1895.

ERSKINE, ALBERT RUSSEL. *History of the Studebaker Corporation*, 1924.

FAULKNER, HAROLD UNDERWOOD, KEPNER, TYLER, AND BART-LETT HALL. *The American Way of Life*, New York, Harper & Brothers, 1941.

FORBES, ESTHER. *Paul Revere and the World He Lived In*, Boston, Houghton Mifflin Co., 1942.

GIBBONS, HERBERT ADAMS, *John Wanamaker* (two volumes), New York, Harper & Brothers, 1926.

GREELEY, HORACE AND OTHERS. *Great Industries of the United States*, Hartford, J. B. Burr & Hyde, 1872.

GLOVER, JOHN GEORGE AND WILLIAM BOOCK CORNELL, *The Development of American Industries*, New York, Prentice-Hall, 1941.

HAMMOND, JOHN WINTHROP, *Men and Volts*, Philadelphia, J. B. Lippincott & Co., 1941.

HITTELL, JOHN S. *The Commerce and Industries of the Pacific Coast*, San Francisco, A. L. Bancroft & Co., 1882.

HILLYER, WILLIAM HOOD, *James Talcott, Merchant, and His Time*, New York, Charles Scribner's Sons, 1932.

HAZARD, BLANCHE EVANS. *The Organization of the Boot and Shoe Industry in Massachusetts before 1875*. Cambridge, Harvard University Press, 1921.

HUNTS, *Merchant Magazine*, New York, 1844.

INGRAM, J. S. *The Centennial Exposition (1876)*, Springfield, Mass. Hubbard Bros., 1876.

INGLIS, WILLIAM. *George F. Johnson, and His Industrial Democracy*, New York, Huntington Press, 1935

JACKSON, JOSEPH HENRY. *Anybody's Gold*, New York, D. Appleton-Century Co., 1941.

KNIGHT, EDWARD H. *Knight's American Mechanical Dictionary* (three volumes), New York, J. B. Ford & Co., 1874.

KELLY, FRED C. *One Thing Leads to Another*, Boston, Houghton Mifflin Co., 1936.

MASSACHUSETTS (*State Guide Series*), Boston, Houghton Mifflin Co., 1937.

MILES, REV. HENRY A. *Lowell as It Was and Is*, Lowell, Powers & Bagley, 1845.

MILLER, JAMES MARTIN. *The Amazing Story of Henry Ford.* 1922.

NEW YORK (*State Guide Series*), New York, Oxford University Press, 1940.

NEW JERSEY (*State Guide Series*), New York, Viking Press, 1939.

Other Industries of New England, Boston, State Street Trust Company.

PENNSYLVANIA (*State Guide Series*), New York, Oxford University Press, 1940.

PERSONS, HERBERT COLLINS. *A Puritan Outpost,* New York, The Macmillan Co., 1937.

ROGERS, AGNES. *From Man to Machine,* Boston, Little, Brown & Co., 1941.

SMITH, J. E. A. *History of Pittsfield (Mass.)* (two volumes,), Springfield, Mass., C. W. Bryon & Co., 1876.

SMITH, HELEN EVERTSON. *Colonial Days and Ways,* New York, The Century Co., 1900.

Some Industries of New England, Boston, State Street Trust Company.

DEABURY, GEORGE J. *Shall Pharmacists Become Tradesmen,* New York. 1899.

TRAIN, ARTHUR, JR. *The Story of Everyday Things.* New York, Harper & Brothers, 1941.

U. S. Patent Office Report for 1844.

U. S. Patent Office Report for 1850.

WALTON, PERRY. *The Story of Textiles,* New York, Tudor Publishing Co., 1925.

WARSHAW, H. T. *Representative Industries in the United States,* New York, Henry Holt & Co., 1928.

WARSHOW, ROBERT IRVING. *Alexander Hamilton, First American Business Man,* Garden City, Garden City Publishing Co., 1931.

WASHBURN, ROBERT COLLYER. *The Life and Times of Lydia E. Pinkham,* New York, G. P. Putnam's Sons, 1931.

WINKLER, JOHN R. *Five and Ten,* New York, Robert M. McBride & Co., 1940.

YATES, RAYMOND F. *Machines Over Men,* New York, Frederick A. Stokes Co., 1939.

INDEX

Lydia E. Pinkham's Vegetable Compound, 150

McCormick, Cyrus Hall, 186f., 189, 212, 233, 235
McCormick, Robert, 186f.
McKay sewing machine for shoes, 236-7
Machine gun, Portable air-cooled, 241
Maizona, 206
Manchester, England, 16, 20
Mansfield, Mass., 232
Marshfield, Mass., 69
Mason & Baldwin, 231
Massachusetts Bay Colony, 68
Matches, The first friction, 167, 233
Matthews, John, 233
Melville, David, 229
Menlo Park, 238
Merchants Magazine, 25
Merino sheep, 228
Mergenthaler, Ottmar, 239f.
Meriden, Conn., 201
Mexico, 125, 155
Milk condensed, 236
Milking machines, 206
Miller, Phineas, 26, 28ff.
Mills, Elisha, 231
Mint, First American, 157f.
Mississippi River, 132
Montague, Mrs. Hannah Lord, 108
Monticello, 84
Moody and Sankey Revival, 149
Morgan & Co., J. P., 240
Morris, Robert, 11, 31
Morse, Prof. H. B., 233f.
Morse telegraph, 192, 202
Motorcars driven by gasoline, 239
Mt. Vernon, 184
Muscatine, Iowa, 239

Nail-making, First attempts at, 20
Napoleon, 177
National City Bank, 230
Needlemaking, 200
Neponset, Mass., 91, 235
Newbold, Charles, 68
Newburyport, Mass., 89, 228, 230
New Haven, Conn., 26, 29, 32, 44, 98

New Orleans La., 132, 236
Newport, R. I., 229
Newspaper advertising, First, 101f.
New York, N. Y., 106, 229
New York Herald, 122ff., 236
New York, New Haven and Hartford Railway, 240
Niagara suspension bridge, 237
North, Lord, 85f., 90
Northern Pacific Railway, 237, 239
Norwich, Conn., 40

Oglethorpe, 13
O'Hara, Col. James, 228
Ohio River, 132
Oil well drilling, 236
One-price policy, Introduction of, 143f.
Opium from China and Iran, 131

Packet, Norwich, 40
Page, G., 235
Panama Canal, 241
Patent Act, Federal, 65
Pattison, Edward, 94
Pattison, William, 94
Pawtucket, R. I., 18, 64
Peck, Epaphroditus, 47f.
Penn, William, 13
Pennsylvania Railroad, 236, 240
Pens, Metallic, 230
Perkins, Jacob, 89, 228, 230
Peru, 155
Phillips, Alonzo D., 233
Phoenix, 230
Pianos with iron frames, 234; Uprights, 237
Pike's Peak, 239
Pilgrim Fathers, 63, 68
Pinckney, 80
Pinmaking, 199, 202
Pitts Brothers, 233
Pittsburgh, Pa., 89
Pittsfield, Mass., 160
Pizarro, 155
Plowmaking, 67ff.
Plymouth, Conn., 41-2
Plymouth Rock, 63
Pocketknives, 234
Pope, Col. A. A., 238